W9-CKT-185

SAVORY
COCKTAILS

SOUR   SPICY   HERBAL   UMAMI   BITTER   SMOKY   RICH   STRONG

GREG HENRY

Ulysses Press

To my mom. She wasn't much of a cocktail drinker, but she did put the letters LUV on the wall above our 1970s freestanding bar in the downstairs den. Then when she got tired of it, she let me move that bar upstairs to my bedroom—which I thought was pretty darn glamorous as a 10-year-old.

Copyright text and photographs © 2013 by Greg Henry. Copyright concept and design © 2013 by Ulysses Press and its licensors. All Rights Reserved. Any unauthorized duplication in whole or in part or dissemination of this edition by any means (including but not limited to photocopying, electronic devices, digital versions, and the Internet) will be prosecuted to the fullest extent of the law.

Published by
ULYSSES PRESS
P.O. Box 3440
Berkeley, CA 94703
www.ulyssespress.com

ISBN: 978-1-61243-222-9
Library of Congress Catalog Number 2013938631

Printed in the United States by Bang Printing

10 9 8 7 6 5 4 3 2 1

Acquisitions Editor: Katherine Furman
Managing Editor: Claire Chun
Editor: Phyllis Elving
Proofreader: Lauren Harrison
Layout: what!design @ whatweb.com
Index: Sayre Van Young
Cover photographs: © Greg Henry

NOTE TO READERS: This book is independently authored and published and no sponsorship or endorsement of this book by, and no affiliation with, any trademarked brand of alcoholic beverages, copyrighted or trademarked characters, or other products mentioned or pictured within is claimed or suggested. All trademarks that appear in ingredient lists and elsewhere in this book belong to their respective owners and are used here for informational purposes only. The authors and publishers encourage readers to patronize the quality brands of alcoholic beverages and other products mentioned in this book.

TABLE OF CONTENTS

INTRO 1

GLASSWARE 2

TOOLS 3

TECHNIQUES 5

SYRUPS 6

Simple Syrup 6

Ginger and Black Pepper
Agave Syrup 7

Clove-Infused Honey Syrup 8

Habanero Agave Syrup 8

Citrus Syrup 8

Oleo-Saccharum 9

BITTERS 9

Aromatic "House" Bitters
of Your Own 10

SHRUBS 10

Pineapple Rosemary Shrub 10

Beet and Juniper Shrub 11

INFUSIONS 12

SOUR 13

Papa Hemingway Daiquiri 15

Biarritz Monk 17

"Monk Buck" from Biarritz 17

My Word 19

Rhubarb Rosemary Flip 21

Green Tea Gimlet 23

Moonlit Night 23

Garden Party Punch 25

Yuzu Sour 27

Golden Ale 28

SPICY 29

Green Gargoyle 31

Vichy Cycle 33

Top Hat 33

Winter Squash 35

Scandi Gibson 37

The Spice Trail 37

Rum-Muddled Diplomat 39

Cool and Starry 39

Burning Sensation 41

Thai Bird Chile Kamikaze 41

Holland Razor Blade 43

Pink Peppercorn Hot Gin Sling 43

Warm Cardigan 44

HERBAL 45

Triple C Collins 47

Breeder's Cup 49

Tom and Daisy 49

Beetle Juice 51

A Savory Cocktail 53

Celery Shrub Cocktail 53

Pimm's Cup Up 55

Greens Fee Fizz 57

To Hell with Spain #2 57

Golden Lion 59

Fennel Fizz 59

Salad Bowl Gin and Tonic 61

Scarborough Fair 61

The Grazer's Edge 63

This Feeling of Joy 64

UMAMI 65

Savory Tomato Juice 67

Bloody Mary 69

Sungold Zinger 71

Tartufo 73

Truffle-Infused Cognac 73

Silk and Gators 75

Dog's Nose 77

Bullshot 77

Black Pepper Oyster Shooters 79

Pork and Beans 79

Pickleback (Make Mine a Double) . . . 80

Homemade Spicy Dill Pickles
and Brine 80

BITTER 81

Bitter Beauty 83

Charentes Shrub 85

Barrel-Aged Berlioni 87

Dead Glamour 89

Black Salt 89

Aperol Tequila Swizzle 91

Off-White Negroni 91

Hanky Panky 92

SMOKY 93

The Long Goodbye 95

Autumn Ash 97

Better with Bacon 97

Smog Cutter 99

Smokejumper 99

The Chaparral 101

The Hickory Stick 103

Old Hickory 103

Rickey Oaxaqueña 105

The Christopher Oaxacan 105

Penicillin Cocktail 106

RICH 107

Campari Alexander 109

The Alexander 109

Cool Revival 111

Dill and Lemon Meringue 111

The Guayabera 113

Amaro Flip 115

Chartreuse and the Chocolate
Factory 116

Cacao Bourbon 116

STRONG 117

A Classic Martini 119

Dry Martini 119

Extra-Dry Martini 119

"Perfect" Martini 119

Smoky Martini 119

Gibson 121

Vesper 121

Hair (Raising) Tonic 123

Neon Rose 125

Scofflaw 127

Dorflinger 127

The Fatal Hour 129

Bijou 129

The Franklin Martini 131

Dirty Birdy 131

French Green Dragon 133

The Widow's Kiss 134

INDEX 136

ACKNOWLEDGMENTS 140

ABOUT THE AUTHOR 140

INTRO

We are in the midst of a cocktail renaissance. It started in the '80s with concoctions like the *Sex in the City* drink of choice, the cosmopolitan, but as this renaissance develops, cocktails are becoming more sophisticated and taking a distinctly savory turn. Today's bartenders are reaching for unexpected ingredients and employing culinary techniques such as infusions and purées to expand and sometimes challenge the palate. Herbs and spices are moving from the kitchen to the bar as more and more bartenders develop cocktails with a "from scratch" approach. Innovative ingredients and modern techniques create new categories of beverages, because there comes a point in life when sweet, pink drinks just don't keep you coming back to the bar.

The trend toward savory cocktails had its start with the Bloody Mary (see page 69) and the beef-based Bullshot (see page 77). These brunch-time favorites pack an umami punch. However, savory is much more than the opposite of sweet. It's not a good idea to just throw a cucumber and a fistful of herbs into the blender and hope for the best; you need to balance the flavor elements. Follow a culinary path as you begin building your cocktail. This book will introduce you to some unexpected directions you may never have considered before.

As an example, a Salad Bowl G&T (see page 61) combines muddled herbs and vegetables with the botanicals already present in gin. All on its own this would make a rather one-note drink, but the balance comes from garden-fresh tomatoes and their sweetly acidic bite. Even a savory cocktail needs the right hint of sweet. Cocktail bitters, too, go a long way in seasoning a drink or providing the final flourish.

In addition to earthy herbs and vegetables, bartenders are incorporating such ingredients as "shrubs" for a tangy flavor. These old-fashioned "drinking vinegars" are being rediscovered for the complex sweet and sour effect they can have when mixed into drinks. A beet and juniper shrub in this book (see page 11) makes a bold impact with scallions and a touch of salt in the crimson-hued Beetle Juice (see page 51).

Savory touches needn't be that dramatic. Subtle influences can nudge many classic cocktails toward the savory end of the scale. Tartufo (see page 73), with its touch of truffle-infused honey, maintains the thinnest veil of something dark and earthy. The pinch of smoked salt in Breeder's Cup (see page 49) rounds out its flavors, adding a decidedly savory boost of umami. Perhaps the most subtle way to build a savory drink involves combining some of the more naturally savory spirits, such as medicinal aquavit and malty genever, with interesting liqueurs—artichoke Cynar, cumin-laced kümmel, and allspice dram, for example. These and other centuries-old formulas have made a comeback as bartenders look to old ingredients to provide a modern sensibility. New interpretations, such as Dead Glamour (see page 89) and Vichy Cycle (see page 33), are challenging to the palate and typically very alcohol-forward, but when sipped slowly there can be no denying their savory complexity.

GLASSWARE

You don't need a lot of glassware to make a great drink. But it's nice to have the basics, because proper presentation adds to the enjoyment of a well-made cocktail.

Coupe (or Saucer) This bowl-shaped Champagne glass is better suited for cocktails than for bubbly, so many bartenders have adopted this classic shape. It should hold between 3 and 6 ounces.

Cocktail Glass This 3- to 6-ounce slope-sided glass is considered the quintessential martini glass. It's ideal for most stirred or shaken cocktails.

Collins Glass There's a fine line between a Collins glass and a highball glass. Typically, a Collins glass is slightly taller and narrower, holding 10 to 14 ounces. It's a good size for drinks served over ice and drinks "topped" with something fizzy. An even taller 16-ounce version is known as a chimney glass.

Highball Glass You'll find this versatile glass in both 8- to 10-ounce and 12- to 14-ounce sizes. I consider it interchangeable with a Collins glass.

Old-Fashioned Glass Short and stocky with a heavy bottom suited to muddling, this glass can vary in size from 4 to 12 ounces (or more). The larger ones are often called double old-fashioned glasses. You'll also see this style called a rocks glass, a tumbler, or a whiskey glass.

Punch Cup Small and rounded, a punch cup often has a handle—though that's not my preference. These hold about 6 to 8 ounces and are (of course) used for punch in conjunction with a punchbowl. But their size and rounded shape make them nice for sipping spirits "neat" as well.

Shot Glass Sturdy in form and simple in shape, this little glass holds 1½ ounces when filled to the top. Large "double" shot glasses can be 2 to 4 ounces and are useful for "shooters."

Wine Glass It's not just for wine. It's also a good all-purpose glass that can simplify your glassware choices when entertaining. Wine glasses work well for highballs, large fruity drinks, and spritzers, with or without ice.

TOOLS

As with most things, making a proper cocktail requires the proper equipment, but this need not be fancy. In fact, some of the bright and shiny accessories on the market aren't well suited to the job. Look for durability, quality, and ease of cleaning. Avoid plastic in most cases. Old-school is fun, but it can have its drawbacks. Consider each tool individually. My tools are hardly a matched set. I've chosen each for the job I intend it to perform. Still, some are vintage, some shiny and fun. I never said a good bar tool wasn't those things; it's just not those things primarily.

Call me a neatnik. The first item I'd place on the essentials list is a good (clean) bar towel—actually two bar towels, one a terrycloth workhorse for wiping down your work area and the second a finely woven, lint-free cotton cloth to keep glassware sparkling.

These are what I consider the other essentials:

Barspoon For stirring, mixing, and scooping ingredients in ½-teaspoon additions. Look for a stainless-steel version with a long, thin handle. The handle is often twisted to assist in mixing when it's rotated back and forth between the palms of your hands, or your fingertips if you're very dexterous.

Boston Shaker This is the classic shaker preferred by most bartenders. It comes in two parts: a pint-size glass and a stainless-steel, slope-sided cup that fits snuggly over the mixing glass to create a sealed shaking chamber.

Bottle Opener/Corkscrew For opening wine and beer bottles, I like the all-in-one variety known as the "waiters corkscrew," comprising a corkscrew coil, a bottle opener, and a blade for removing foil, wax, or plastic seals.

Citrus Extractor You can get fancy here; there are mountable bar-top versions that handle everything from the tiniest kumquat to the hugest pomelo. But I like the efficiency of the smaller, handheld metal press version. It comes in chrome, enameled steel, or lightweight but sturdy cast aluminum.

Cutting Board with Paring Knife and/or Small, Serrated Knife Essential and self-explanatory.

Grater The small Microplane version grates nutmeg, chocolate, and citrus zest more finely than the citrus stripper/zester—a welcome addition for finishing drinks with finesse.

Ice Scoop Trust me, make enough cocktails and you'll get frostbitten fingers without one of these. It should be sized to nearly fill a pint glass in a single scoop.

Jigger Look for a dual-cup stainless-steel version. One side is a 1-ounce "pony shot," and the other side holds a 1½-ounce "standard shot," or "jigger." You may also want to have a glass jigger with calibrated measurements for very accurate small additions of liquid.

Mixing Glass If you have a Boston shaker, a mixing glass isn't actually essential. But a nice mixing glass (shiny, crystal, or otherwise fancy) is fun to have. So go ahead and get one.

Muddler The wooden version is classic, but there are many styles that get the job done. Just make sure the handle is long enough and the blunt end is small enough to work well in the tallest of tall (skinny) cocktails.

Strainers: Hawthorne, Julep, and Fine-Mesh Sieve The Hawthorne strainer is the most common style for cocktails and mixed drinks. It should have a stainless-steel head with a spring coil that assists in making a snug fit and keeping ice and other ingredients in the mixing glass. A julep strainer is a large, perforated round spoon. It can be a bit more awkward to use, but with practice you'll find it a good choice for drinks that are stirred in a mixing glass. My rule of thumb is this: when straining a cocktail from the metal cup of a Boston shaker, I choose the Hawthorne; when straining from a smaller mixing glass or the pint glass of a Boston shaker, I choose the julep. The fine-mesh sieve is used in conjunction with either the Hawthorne or julep for double-straining drinks that have been muddled or have fine particles (including ice shards) that aren't part of the final presentation.

TECHNIQUES

Ice is essential to a well-made cocktail. I like medium-size square cubes for stirring, shaking, and serving most drinks "on the rocks." A single extra-large ice cube is best for some very strong drinks that are sipped slowly, because it keeps the drink chilled without diluting it too much. Cracked ice is best for blender drinks and some specialty cocktails.

SHAKEN OR STIRRED?

The basic rule is simple: drinks made with spirits only, such as martinis and manhattans, should be stirred. This introduces less air into the mixture, creating a silky, viscous texture. A well-stirred cocktail starts in a mixing glass or the metal half of a Boston shaker that's half-filled with medium ice cubes (about 5 or 6 of them). Use a long-handled barspoon to gently stir the ingredients until a light frosting appears on the glass and the drink is properly diluted, about 20 seconds.

Shaking is a more aggressive form of mixing, mostly reserved for drinks with juice or other heavy ingredients, such as eggs and cream. It lightens the mixture by adding tiny air bubbles and thin shards of broken ice that will melt into the cocktail. To shake, add a pint-size glassful of ice cubes to the shaker, filling it about ⅔ full. Cover the shaker with its cap, or in the case of a Boston shaker with its pint glass. Grasp with both hands, using one hand to hold the cap or glass securely; shake vigorously until the shaker surface becomes frosty, about 20 to 30 seconds. Remove the cap and quickly strain the drink into a glass.

MEASURING YOUR INGREDIENTS

Use a measuring device that has increments you are comfortable using. I always doubt bartenders who just "eye" the ingredients as they build a drink. I have to wonder how consistent their results are from drink to drink.

Here are conversions for typical bar measurements:

Drop = 1 drop from an eye dropper (not a shaker top)

Dash = ¼ barspoon = ⅛ teaspoon = ⅔ ml

Barspoon = ½ teaspoon = 2½ ml

1 pony shot = 1 fl oz = 30 ml

1 shot (jigger) = 1½ fl oz = 45 ml

1 teaspoon = 8 dashes = 5 ml

1 tablespoon = 3 teaspoons = ½ fl oz = 15 ml

1 cup = ½ pint = 8 fl oz = 8 pony shots = 5⅓ shots = 250 ml

1 pint = 2 cups = 16 fl oz = 16 pony shots = 10⅔ shots = 500 ml

1 quart = 4 cups = 32 fl oz = 32 pony shots = 21⅓ shots = 1,000 ml

SYRUPS

I don't care how savory a cocktail is, most well-made drinks require a sweet element for real balance. Handmade syrups are a great way to explore the possibilities. Sometimes a basic simple syrup of water and sugar is just the right choice. The variations I've given here can bring something unexpected to your creation. Experiment. Taste each syrup after you make it and add sweetener if you feel it's too strong, but keep in mind that the syrup is just one layer in a cocktail; don't dilute its power too much.

SIMPLE SYRUP

1 cup sugar
1 cup water

Stir together the sugar and water in a medium saucepan over medium-high heat. Bring to a boil, stirring occasionally until the sugar is dissolved. Reduce the heat to low and continue cooking until a syrupy consistency is reached, about 4 minutes. Remove from the heat and let stand for 30 minutes. The syrup may be refrigerated and stored in an airtight container for up to 1 month. *This recipe and its variations makes about 1¼ cups each*

SIMPLE SYRUP VARIATIONS

GINGER Once the simple syrup mixture boils, add 2 tablespoons freshly grated ginger; continue cooking as above. Strain through a wire-mesh sieve double-lined with damp cheesecloth, discarding the solids. Store refrigerated in an airtight container for up to 1 month.

HERBAL LEMON Once the simple syrup mixture boils, add 2 thin lemon slices and 1 to 2 tablespoons fresh herbs of any type or combination (such as mint, rosemary, basil, or lemon verbena), to taste. Continue cooking as above. Strain through a wire-mesh sieve double-lined with damp cheesecloth, discarding the solids. Store refrigerated in an airtight container for up to 1 month.

LEMONGRASS KAFFIR Once the simple syrup mixture boils, add 2 tablespoons minced fresh lemongrass (white and light parts only) and 6 bruised kaffir leaves (or substitute the zest of 1 lime for the kaffir leaves). Continue cooking as above. Strain through a wire-mesh sieve lined with a double layer of damp cheesecloth, discarding the solids. Store refrigerated in an airtight container for up to 1 month.

RHUBARB ROSEMARY Once the simple syrup mixture boils, add 2 or 3 rhubarb stalks, sliced. Continue cooking as above. Remove from the heat and add 1 fresh rosemary sprig; let stand 30 minutes. Strain through a wire-mesh sieve lined with a double layer of damp cheesecloth, discarding the solids. Store refrigerated in an airtight container for up to 1 month.

SPICED Once the simple syrup mixture boils, add 1 ounce lightly cracked whole spice, bark, beans, or seeds (about ¼ cup) in any combination (such as allspice, cloves, peppercorns, or coffee), to taste. Continue cooking as above. Strain through a wire-mesh sieve lined with a double layer of damp cheesecloth, discarding the solids. Store refrigerated in an airtight container for up to 1 month.

GINGER AND BLACK PEPPER AGAVE SYRUP

2 ounces thinly sliced fresh ginger (about ½ cup)
2 tsp whole black peppercorns
½ cup warm water
½ cup agave nectar, plus more if needed

Place the ginger slices and peppercorns in a small, nonreactive container and lightly crush them with a bar muddler. Add the warm water and agave nectar; stir to combine and then set aside for about 2 hours to let the flavors come together. Taste the syrup and add more agave nectar if you feel it's too strong.

When your syrup has the taste you want, pour it through a wire-mesh sieve lined with a double layer of damp cheesecloth; discard the solids. Cover and chill. The syrup may be stored in the refrigerator for up to a month, but be warned: ginger loses its potency quickly. Taste before using.   *Makes about 1 cup*

CLOVE-INFUSED HONEY SYRUP

2 tbsp whole cloves

½ cup warm water

½ cup honey

Place the cloves in a small, nonreactive container and lightly crush them with a wooden muddler. Add the warm water and honey; stir to combine, then cover and set aside at room temperature for 2 or 3 days. Taste the syrup; add more honey if you feel it's too strong.

When your syrup has the taste you want, pour it through a wire-mesh sieve lined with a double layer of damp cheesecloth; discard the solids. Store refrigerated in an airtight container for up to 1 month.   *Makes about 1 cup*

HABANERO AGAVE SYRUP

1 habanero chile, thinly sliced

½ cup warm water

½ cup agave nectar, plus more to taste

Place the habanero with all its seeds in a small, nonreactive container. Add the warm water and agave nectar; stir to combine and then set aside for about 1 hour to let the flavors come together. Taste the syrup and add more agave nectar if you feel it's too hot.

When the syrup has the desired heat level, strain it through a wire-mesh sieve double-lined with damp cheesecloth. Store refrigerated in an airtight container for up to 1 month.   *Makes about 1 cup*

CITRUS SYRUP

2 cups sugar

¾ cup freshly squeezed citrus juice (such as lemon, lime, orange, or yuzu*)

¼ cup water

1 tbsp grated citrus zest (such as lemon, lime, orange, or yuzu*)

* For information about yuzu, see page 28.

Stir the ingredients together in a medium saucepan over medium-high heat. Bring to a boil, stirring occasionally until the sugar is dissolved. Lower the heat to low and continue cooking until a syrupy consistency is achieved, about 4 minutes. Remove from the heat and let stand for 30 minutes. Strain through a wire-mesh sieve double-lined with damp cheesecloth. Store refrigerated in an airtight container for up to 1 month. *Makes about 1½ cups*

OLEO-SACCHARUM

6 lemons
1½ cups sugar
¾ cup water

Use a vegetable peeler to remove the skin from the lemons, leaving behind the white pith. In a large bowl, cover the lemon peels with the sugar and toss to combine. Using a muddler or wooden spoon, press the peels to express their oils. Let sit for about an hour, then scrape the mixture into a saucepan. Add the water and bring to a simmer over medium-low heat, stirring occasionally. Once the sugar has dissolved, remove from the heat and let cool. Strain through a wire-mesh sieve double-lined with damp cheesecloth. Store refrigerated in an airtight container for up to 1 month. *Makes about 1½ cups*

BITTERS

If you've ever had even a half-hearted interest in cocktails, you probably have a bottle of bitters lying around. I'd bet it's that yellow-capped bottle wrapped in an oversize paper label and known as Angostura bitters. But there's more to the world of bitters, and this is a great time to explore what they are and what they can do for your cocktails. More varieties of commercially produced bitters are available than ever before. But just what the heck are they?

Cocktail bitters can best be described as something you add in dashes and drops to "season" a drink, integrating ingredients and accentuating flavors—the way salt and pepper enhances food. Bitters are an essential ingredient in classic cocktails and are playing an increasingly important role in modern mixology. They are typically made by infusing botanicals such as herbs, spices, seeds, peels, barks, and roots into some sort of very high-proof alcohol. The flavor combinations can be endless, opening the door to creativity in a huge way.

Bitters weren't always just the creative finishing touch on a well-made cocktail. Originally they were potable elixirs designed as cures for all that ails you. Once bitters became accepted as a form of "medicine," all that was needed was a palatable way to deliver them. Enter the cocktail.

There are a number of bitters used in this book that you may not be able to find at your local liquor store, but they are easily purchased online at retailers such as Amazon. But if you want a truly personal cocktail, go ahead and experiment with making your own.

AROMATIC "HOUSE" BITTERS OF YOUR OWN

1 lemon

1 orange

¼ cup dried currants, cranberries, or cherries

3 whole cardamom pods, lightly cracked

1 (2-inch) piece cinnamon stick

1 tsp coriander seeds

1 whole star anise

8 to 10 drops gentian extract (available online)

2 cups 100-proof rye

1 tbsp simple syrup (see page 6)

Use a vegetable peeler to remove the lemon and orange zest in thin strips, leaving the white pith behind. Place the zest, dried fruit, cardamom, cinnamon, coriander, star anise, gentian extract, and rye in a quart jar that has a tight-fitting lid. Cover and store in a dark place at room temperature for 2 weeks, shaking or rolling the jar every other day. Then strain the liquid through a fine-mesh sieve double-lined with cheesecloth into a 2 or 3-cup pitcher. Stir in the simple syrup. Funnel your bitters into small bottles that have squeeze-dropper caps. Will keep in a cool, dark place indefinitely. *Makes about 2 cups*

SHRUBS

Shrubs are old-fashioned drinking vinegars that are becoming noticed again as flavorful ingredients in both sweet and savory cocktails. Shrubs are also excellent simply mixed with seltzer or club soda and served over ice.

PINEAPPLE ROSEMARY SHRUB

¼ pineapple, peeled, cored, and cut into ½-inch slices (sized to fit your container)

¾ cup / 6 fl oz apple cider vinegar, or more as needed

½ cup sugar

1 large fresh rosemary sprig

Place the pineapple slices in a wide-mouth jar that has a lid. Add enough cider vinegar to cover the fruit completely. Cover the jar and let the vinegar infuse for 4 days, gently shaking or rolling the jar each day. Strain the liquid through a fine-mesh sieve double lined with damp cheesecloth into a small, nonreactive saucepan. Add the sugar and bring to a boil. Lower the heat, add the rosemary, and simmer for 10 minutes. Remove from the heat and strain once more. Allow to cool completely before bottling. Store refrigerated in an airtight container for up to 1 month. *Makes a generous ½ cup*

BEET AND JUNIPER SHRUB

20 baby beets
¾ cup / 6 fl oz apple cider vinegar
¾ cup / 6 fl oz water
½ cup sugar
½ tsp kosher salt
1 tbsp whole black peppercorns
1 tbsp whole juniper berries

Trim and peel the beets to a uniform size, about as big as a large olive; set aside. In a small, nonreactive saucepan, combine the vinegar, water, sugar, salt, peppercorns, and juniper berries; stir until the sugar is dissolved. Add the beets and set over high heat to bring to a boil. Reduce the heat to low and simmer, swirling the pan occasionally and turning the beets, until the beets are tender, about 25 minutes.

Use a slotted spoon to transfer the beets to a small container that has a cover. Raise the heat under the saucepan to medium and reduce the liquid to 1 cup. Remove from the heat, let come to room temperature, and strain into the same container as the beets, discarding the peppercorns and juniper berries. Refrigerate the shrub and beets together, covered, for up to 3 weeks. *Makes 20 pickled beets plus 1 cup shrub*

INFUSIONS

Making your own infusions is an easy, enjoyable expression of the art of the cocktail. You can steep any spirit you like, but regardless of the base spirit and flavor infusions you choose, the general idea remains the same: the key to success is to experiment and taste as you go.

Most infusions need 3 to 5 days in a dark place to attain the right flavor profile. Some flavors (such as seeds and nuts) will take longer, while chile pepper infusions only need a few hours to get fiery hot. No equipment is needed other than a clean, sealable container, though steeping them in a dark place such as a cupboard is best. Most ingredients should be sliced, chopped, or lightly crushed to assist in the flavor transfer. All infusions should be well strained before use.

I used 2 cups of vodka for the following examples, but feel free to halve or double (or quadruple) my guidelines. Infusions keep at room temperature for up to 1 month or can be frozen for up to 2 months, unless otherwise indicated.

CITRUS INFUSION Infuse 2 cups base spirit with 1 cup citrus peels for at least 48 hours, swirling the container occasionally.

HERBAL INFUSION Infuse 2 cups base spirit with 1 cup loosely packed herbs for 3 to 4 weeks, swirling the container occasionally.

HOT CHILE PEPPER INFUSION Infuse 2 cups base spirit with ½ cup sliced chiles (such as serrano, jalapeño, or Thai bird) for 1 to 4 hours (or to taste), swirling the container occasionally.

BLACK PEPPERCORN INFUSION Infuse 2 cups base spirit with ¼ cup whole black peppercorns for 24 to 48 hours, swirling the container occasionally.

COFFEE INFUSION Infuse 2 cups base spirit with ¼ cup roasted and lightly cracked dark espresso bean for 24 to 48 hours, swirling the container occasionally.

GINGER INFUSION Infuse 2 cups base spirit with ¼ cup thinly sliced fresh ginger for 24 to 48 hours, swirling the container occasionally.

MILD-FLAVORED VEGETABLE INFUSION Infuse 2 cups base spirit with 1 cup chopped vegetables such as celery and cucumber and 1 dried bay leaf for 2 to 3 weeks, swirling the container occasionally.

STRONG-FLAVORED VEGETABLE INFUSION Infuse 2 cups base spirit with 1 cup chopped vegetables such as beets and squash (raw or roasted, as you prefer) for 5 to 7 days, swirling the container occasionally.

SEED OR NUT INFUSION Most seeds or nuts should be roasted before infusion, then lightly cracked. Infuse 2 cups base spirit with 1 cup seeds or nuts (such as hazelnuts) for 2 to 3 weeks, swirling the container occasionally.

WHOLE SPICE INFUSION Most whole spices—such as allspice, anise, cinnamon, clove, or cumin—should be roasted before infusion, then lightly cracked. Infuse 2 cups base spirit with ¼ cup spices for 24 to 48 hours, swirling the container occasionally.

SOUR

Sour cocktails are fresh, bright, and tangy, with clean—often citrusy—aromas. They make wonderful aperitifs. Their sharp flavors stimulate the appetite, letting you know that dinner will soon follow.

Sailors of the early British navy may have unknowingly originated this style of cocktail. They were given rations of lime juice to help fight off scurvy, a disease caused by a lack of vitamin C. Sailors being sailors, as the story goes, they began to mix their sour fruit rations with standard-issue rum or gin—leading to a whole range of classics, including the whiskey sour, Tom Collins, and eventually the margarita and daiquiri.

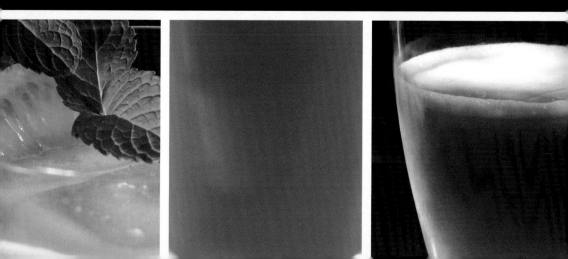

PAPA HEMINGWAY DAIQUIRI

You don't have to be a reader to know that novelist Ernest Hemingway was a man who liked to drink. It's no wonder he tinkered with Cuba's classic Daiquiri while he was on the island in the 1950s. It's been said that he followed a "12-a-day rule," mostly while he sat "working" at the bar at *La Florida* in Havana. According to the memoir of journalist and longtime friend A. E. Hotchner, the Papa Hemingway "was compounded of two and a half jiggers of Bacardi White Label Rum, the juice of two limes, and half a grapefruit and six drops of maraschino." That's way more sour and way stronger than the original—a subtle blend of lime and rum—and is befitting a man with big tastes.

2 shots / 90 ml / 3 fl oz clear rum
1½ tbsp / ¾ fl oz freshly squeezed lime juice
1 tbsp / ½ fl oz freshly squeezed grapefruit juice
¼ pony shot / 7½ ml / ¼ fl oz maraschino liqueur
1⅓ cups / 10½-oz glassful of ice (for the frozen version)
1 lime wedge, as garnish

Shaken and strained: Add the rum, lime juice, grapefruit juice, and maraschino liqueur to a cocktail shaker half-filled with ice. Shake vigorously until well chilled. Strain into a chilled coupe or cocktail glass and garnish with a masculine hunk of lime.

Frozen: Place everything except the lime in a blender and blend thoroughly. Pour into an extra-large chilled coupe or cocktail glass. Garnish with lime. *Makes 1*

Tip
For frozen drinks, I like the Vitamix Barboss blender. I'd blend this drink on the #3 setting.

BIARRITZ MONK

I got the idea for this Biarritz Monk cocktail from *Around the World with Jigger, Beaker, and Flask* by Charles Henry Baker, Jr. (1939). His version is called Monk Buck from Biarritz. Bucks are a style of cocktail that have been slung across bars since the 1890s. Besides a base spirit and something sour, they typically include ginger ale. I love the interplay between ginger and cognac, but ginger ale is far too sweet for my taste. (And as much as I love his book, it seems I'm never wholly satisfied with his drinks as written.) So I left the "buck" out and began to experiment. By the time I was finished, I had a fragrant cocktail that's a bit pungent and plenty sour.

1 thin slice fresh ginger
2 pony shots / 60 ml / 2 fl oz cognac
2 tbsp / 1 fl oz freshly squeezed lemon juice
1½ tbsp / ¾ fl oz ginger and black pepper agave syrup (see page 7)
½ pony shot / 15 ml / ½ fl oz yellow Chartreuse
1 large, wide lemon peel chip, as garnish

Rub the ginger slice along the rim of a big, heavy double old-fashioned glass. Drop the ginger into the glass and add an extra-large ice cube. Set aside.

In a mixing glass half-filled with ice, combine the cognac, lemon juice, ginger and black pepper agave syrup, and Chartreuse. Stir until chilled and properly diluted, about 20 seconds. Julep-strain into the prepared glass. Garnish with the lemon chip, expressing its oil onto the surface, rubbing it onto the rim of the glass, and dropping it in the drink, peel side up. *Makes 1*

"MONK BUCK" FROM BIARRITZ

This is a more faithful interpretation of the original.

1 long, thin strip lemon peel
2 pony shots / 60 ml / 2 fl oz cognac
½ cup / 4 fl oz ginger ale
½ pony shot / 30 ml / ½ fl oz yellow Chartreuse

Place the lemon peel strip in a Collins or highball glass; fill the glass with cracked ice. Add the cognac and ginger ale; pour in the Chartreuse over a barspoon, drizzling it onto the ice. *Makes 1*

MY WORD

Yes, this is a riff on the cocktail The Last Word (sometimes called The Final Word). Despite its on-again-off-again popularity, this is really quite a drink: sour, pungent, even a bit rich. It seems to have originated in the 1920s at the Detroit Athletic Club, where it became very popular. Then came Prohibition . . . and away went some of this country's best cocktails, the original version of this drink among them. Luckily, it made a little comeback in 1951 when it was published in Ted Saucier's classic cocktail book *Bottoms Up!* But as the clock kept ticking, the drink was lost to history again until Murray Stenson, while behind the bar at Seattle's Zig Zag Café, brought it back to our attention. It's currently favored in one version or another in discerning cocktail bars all over the country.

I tried to imagine what this cocktail would have been like with the older-style gin used in pre-Prohibition America. Ransom's Old Tom gin nicely fills that niche for me. The egg white was an impulse; I think it adds a bit of textural elegance.

2 pony shots / 60 ml / 2 fl oz Ransom or other Old Tom gin
½ pony shot / 30 ml / ½ fl oz green Chartreuse
½ pony shot / 30 ml / ½ fl oz maraschino liqueur
1 tbsp / ½ fl oz freshly squeezed lemon juice
1 small egg white (optional)
1 mint sprig, as garnish
1 lemon wheel, as garnish

Pour the gin, Chartreuse, maraschino liqueur, lemon juice, and egg white (if using) into a cocktail shaker. Cover and vigorously "dry shake" for about 30 seconds to combine. Uncap, fill the shaker ⅔ full with medium ice cubes, and shake vigorously again until frothy, at least 30 seconds. Using a Hawthorn strainer, double-strain the cocktail through a wire-mesh sieve over one extra-large ice cube into a double old-fashioned glass. Wait a moment for the foam to rise, then garnish with the mint sprig and lemon wheel. *Makes 1*

RHUBARB ROSEMARY FLIP

Rhubarb, rhubarb, rhubarb—that's not me muttering to myself, but it is fun to say. It's especially fun when you say Rhubarb Rosemary Flip. I bet its creator, Carol Donovan, is fun, too—with her résumé of gigs singing classical music all over Chicago. I imagine her singing behind the bar when she developed this drink for Chicago restaurant The Hearty Boys.

The heart of this drink is a rhubarb and rosemary syrup, a ruby-red handmade elixir that packs a sweet and sour punch. I'm sure you know rhubarb—that tart red stalk usually associated with dessert pies and cobblers. It's a charmingly "old-fashioned" ingredient that has somehow resisted mass-market appeal, but Carol's syrup brings it into the modern age. It's terrific when paired with the botanicals in gin.

1 shot / 45 ml / 1½ fl oz dry gin
1½ tbsp / ¾ fl oz rhubarb rosemary syrup (see page 7), plus more for drizzling
1½ tbsp / ¾ fl oz freshly squeezed lime juice
1 small egg white (optional)
1 long fresh rosemary sprig, as garnish

Pour the gin, rhubarb rosemary syrup, lime juice, and egg white (if using) into a cocktail shaker. Cover and vigorously "dry shake" for about 30 seconds to combine. Add enough medium ice cubes to nearly fill the shaker, cover, and shake as vigorously as you can until frothy, at least 30 seconds. Strain into an ice-filled tall Collins or chimney glass. Drizzle or drop another ¼ oz (½ tbsp) of the rhubarb rosemary syrup over the top. Garnish with the rosemary. *Makes 1*

Tip

Does the idea of an egg in your cocktail make you a bit queasy? Well, relax. A raw egg white helps unify flavors; what it doesn't do is add an eggy taste or create a slimy texture. In fact, a properly shaken egg white creates a soft, silky foam that rises to the top of the cocktail.

Still, many people raise their eyebrows at the thought of raw eggs. Raw eggs have been somewhat vilified, and while it's true that raw eggs carry some risk of salmonella, with properly stored fresh eggs the risk is very, very low. Pasteurized eggs remove the threat entirely. But if you're still not sure, all I can say is that you're really missing out.

GREEN TEA GIMLET

My Green Tea Gimlet is the perfect party cocktail, so I like to make it by the pitcherful. You can file this under Party Planning 101 and thank me later, because serving cocktails by the pitcher to a crowd is not only convenient, it's super-smart quality control.

1½ cups / 12 fl oz dry gin, at room temperature
2 green tea bags
¾ cup / 6 fl oz freshly squeezed lime juice
4 to 6 tbsp / 2 to 3 fl oz citrus syrup made with lemon, to taste (see page 8)
6 lime wedges, as garnish

Make the base: Pour the gin into a 3-cup or larger pitcher. Add the tea bags and let sit at room temperature for at least 1 hour. When ready to serve, remove the tea bags and add the lime juice and citrus syrup; stir until well combined.

Make the cocktails: For each cocktail, add about 3¼ ounces of the base to a cocktail shaker ⅔ filled with ice. Cover and shake vigorously; strain into an ice-filled old-fashioned glass. Squeeze a lime wedge over the drink and drop it in. *Makes 6*

MOONLIT NIGHT

This drink was created by Stephan Berg from The Bitter Truth, a cocktail bitters company. It's based on a classic Aviation cocktail and was created as a romantic gesture toward a woman. She was impressed by its pale blue color, saying it reminded her of the poem "Mondnacht" (Moonlit Night). Needless to say, the date was a success. Even a savory book has to have a sweet story.

2 pony shots / 60 ml / 2 fl oz tequila blanco
½ pony shot / 15 ml / ½ fl oz The Bitter Truth or other violet liqueur
½ pony shot / 15 ml / ½ fl oz maraschino liqueur
2 tbsp / 1 fl oz freshly squeezed lime Juice
2 or 3 dashes orange bitters
1 small egg white (optional)

Add the tequila, violet, maraschino, lime juice, bitters, and egg white (if using) to a cocktail shaker. Cover and vigorously "dry shake" for about 30 seconds to combine. Uncap the shaker and fill ⅔ full with medium ice cubes, then shake vigorously again until frothy, at least 30 seconds. Using a Hawthorn strainer, double-strain the cocktail through a wire-mesh sieve into a chilled cocktail glass. *Makes 1*

GARDEN PARTY PUNCH

Every party should have a punch, and this one has an old-fashioned appeal that's perfect for a modern-day party. It comes from Nathan Hazard, one of my podcast partners at *The Table Set*.

3 cups chopped rhubarb
3 tbsp sugar
1 (750 ml) bottle dry gin
Distilled water, as needed
1 lemon, sliced into wheels
2 cups oleo-saccharum (see page 9)
2½ cups / 20 fl oz freshly squeezed red grapefruit juice
1½ cups / 12 fl oz freshly squeezed lemon juice
1½ cups / 12 fl oz Lillet Rose
12 dashes Fee Brothers rhubarb bitters (available online, optional)
1 liter club soda
Peels from 3 grapefruit (use a vegetable peeler to avoid the pith)
2 or 3 fresh rosemary sprigs, as garnish

Make the infusion: Place the rhubarb and sugar in a large wide-mouth glass jar or bowl; let macerate for at least 1 hour. Add the gin, cover, and place in a cool, dark place. Let the gin infuse for about 2 weeks (or to taste), swirling the container occasionally. Strain through a fine-mesh sieve lined with a double layer of damp cheesecloth.

Prepare the ice: In a large pot, bring distilled water to a boil; you'll need enough to fill a metal bowl or bundt pan several inches smaller in diameter than your punch bowl. Cool and chill in the refrigerator. Arrange lemon wheels and rosemary in the bottom of the bowl or bundt pan, saving some of the rosemary for garnish. Pour in chilled distilled water to cover the lemons by about ½ inch. Cover and freeze until set. Then fill the mold with more chilled distilled water so that it comes to 1 inch below the rim. Cover with plastic wrap and freeze overnight.

Make the punch: Combine the oleo-saccharum, rhubarb-infused gin, grapefruit juice, lemon juice, Lillet Rose, rhubarb bitters (if using), and grapefruit peels in a large pitcher. Cover and refrigerate for at least 4 hours.

When ready to serve, dip the bottom of the ice mold into a bowl of hot water to loosen it, then transfer the ice into your punch bowl, lemon side up. Pour in the chilled punch; add the club soda and garnish with grapefruit peels and remaining rosemary. *Makes about 20 cups*

YUZU SOUR

For this Yuzu Sour I propose pisco, a brandy blended from several different grape varieties common to South America. Both Peru and Chile produce excellent piscos. While either of these would work well for this recipe, I've styled the drink after Peru's full-bodied, tangy citrus Pisco Sour—undoubtedly their iconic national cocktail. My version features yuzu, a super-sour citrus that gives it a decidedly Japanese flair. This may seem globally out of sync, but in truth Peru was the first nation to establish diplomatic relations with Japan. As a result, there is a long history of Japanese immigration to that South American country.

2 shots / 90 ml / 3 fl oz pisco
2 tbsp / 1 fl oz yuzu juice, freshly squeezed or bottled*
½ pony shot / 15 ml / ½ fl oz ginger liqueur
1 small egg white (optional)
4 drops Miracle Mile yuzu bitters (available online, optional)

* Lime juice may be substituted for yuzu juice. For more information about yuzu, see the Golden Ale recipe on page 28.

Combine the pisco, yuzu juice, ginger liqueur, and egg white (if using) in a cocktail shaker. Cover and vigorously "dry shake" for about 30 seconds to combine. Don't skip this step—it really helps build structure. In fact, the longer and more vigorously you shake, the more lift you'll get from the foam that's created. Uncap the shaker and fill with medium ice cubes ⅔ full; shake vigorously again until frothy, at least 30 seconds. Using a Hawthorn strainer, double-strain the cocktail through a wire-mesh sieve into a chilled old-fashioned glass. Wait a moment for the foam to rise and then place 4 drops of bitters (if using) in a circle on top. Use the tip of a skewer to connect the dots. *Makes 1*

GOLDEN ALE

Riffs are modern cocktails inspired by classics. Gabriella Mlynarczyk, from Chef Michael Voltaggio's Ink restaurant in Los Angeles, presents one here that can be best described as a Belgian Michelada or a spicy take on a Shandy.

1 lemon wedge

Sea salt as needed, preferably smoked

1 scant barspoon hot sauce

2 pony shots / 60 ml / 2 fl oz vodka

½ pony shot / 15 ml / ½ fl oz elderflower liqueur

½ fl oz yuzu juice, freshly squeezed or bottled*

1 tbsp / ½ fl oz lemon juice

1 tbsp / ½ oz honey syrup (honey and warm water in a 1:1 ratio)

4 to 6 tbsp / 2 to 3 fl oz Belgian-style golden ale

* Yuzu is a very aromatic sour citrus fruit that originated in East Asia. It's typical in Japanese cooking and integral to ponzu sauce. Yuzu can be found in-season at many Asian markets, or it can be purchased as bottled juice in Asian markets or online. Lime juice can be substituted.

Use the lemon wedge to lightly moisten the rim of a highball glass. Pour the salt onto a small saucer, spreading it out in a thin, even layer. Press the rim into the salt, cookie-cutter style, twisting it back and forth to get an evenly coated rim. Fill the glass with medium ice cubes; set aside.

To a cocktail shaker ⅔ filled with ice, add the hot sauce, vodka, elderflower liqueur, yuzu juice, lemon juice, and honey syrup. Cover and shake. Strain into the prepared glass and top with ale. *Makes 1*

SPICY

Would you rather be too hot or too cold? Don't sweat it. Spicy cocktails are both hot and cold. As illogical as it sounds, piquant spices can help cool you down. The cuisines of Thailand and Mexico illustrate this theory, and I say it works with drinks, too. Whether they're made fiery with jalapeños or a bit tamer with cayenne, there's an art to finding the balance that tingles the tongue but cools the brow.

In this chapter I also hope to prove that there's more to spice than red hot chile peppers. When the weather cools, spices such as nutmeg, cinnamon, allspice, caraway, and even cumin offer warm comfort.

GREEN GARGOYLE

The spice in this cocktail proves that you needn't be afraid of a little fire when it comes to liquid refreshment. I was given this recipe by my friend Linda Miller Nicholson, the woman behind the blog *Salty Seattle*. She also leads a series of intimate culinary retreats east of Seattle, where it may get chilly but she sure loves the heat.

1 tbsp salt, preferably Hawaiian alaea pink salt

1 lime wedge

1 (1-inch) piece unpeeled English cucumber, quartered

2 or 3 thin rounds fresh jalapeño, to taste, plus more as garnish

3 or 4 fresh cilantro sprigs (leaves only), plus more as garnish

2 tbsp / 1 fl oz freshly squeezed lime juice

1 tbsp / ½ fl oz agave syrup*

2 pony shots / 60 ml / 2 fl oz tequila blanco

Mix agave nectar and water in a 1:1 ratio.

Using a mortar and pestle, crush the salt until it is the texture of coarse sand. Press the lime wedge onto a section of the glass rim to create a half-moon impression. Tip the mortar gathering the salt on one side and roll the moist section of the glass in the salt so the salt adheres. Place 1 large or 3 medium ice cubes in the glass; set aside.

In a sturdy, thick-bottomed pint glass from a Boston shaker, use a bar muddler to crush the cucumber, jalapeño, cilantro, lime juice, and agave syrup into a fragrant, pulpy mush. Add the tequila and swirl to combine.

Fill the metal part of the Boston shaker ⅔ full with ice. Pour the muddled tequila mixture (including pulp) over the ice, then cap the shaker with the pint glass. Shake vigorously until well chilled. Uncap and use a Hawthorn strainer to double-strain the cocktail through a wire-mesh sieve into the prepared glass. Float additional jalapeño slices on top, to taste. Garnish with more cilantro sprigs. *Makes 1*

VICHY CYCLE

The *Zig Zag Café* in Seattle is my kind of bar—first, because it's so hard to find, and second, because once you find it you'll never forget it. Arguably, it landed on the map thanks to Murray Stensen, known to his regular customers as "The Blur." Today the bar is still in able hands with Erik Hakkinen. Erik served me the Vichy Cycle, a cocktail of his own creation. Erik handles its boldness with dexterity in this collaboration between French vermouth and German kümmel.

2 pony shots / 60 ml / 2 fl oz calvados
1 pony shot / 30 ml / 1 fl oz white vermouth
½ pony shot / 15 ml / ½ fl oz kümmel
2 dashes Aromatic "House" Bitters (see page 10), or The Bitter Truth Jerry Thomas'
    Own Decanter Bitters (available online)
1 lemon twist, as garnish

Combine the calvados, vermouth, kümmel, and bitters in a mixing glass half-filled with ice. Stir until chilled and properly diluted, about 20 seconds. Julep-strain into chilled coupe or cocktail glass. Garnish with a lemon twist, expressing its oil onto the surface, rubbing it on the rim of the glass, and dropping it in, peel side up. *Makes 1*

TOP HAT

The Top Hat from Ira Koplowitz of Bittercube cocktail bitters, is another cocktail featuring kümmel. This liqueur is practically unheard of in North America, but the Brits enjoy it. It even makes an appearance in Ian Fleming's novel *Goldfinger*, when "tough cheery men" quaff double kümmels after lunch.

1 shot / 45 ml / 1½ fl oz brandy
1½ tbsp / ¾ fl oz freshly squeezed lime juice
1 tbsp / ⅓ fl oz kümmel
1½ tsp / ¼ fl oz maraschino liqueur
1 tbsp / ½ fl oz simple syrup (see page 6)
1 dash orange bitters
1 orange twist, as garnish

In a cocktail shaker ⅔ filled with ice, combine the brandy, lime juice, kümmel, maraschino liqueur, simple syrup, and bitters. Cover and shake. Strain into a chilled coupe glass. Garnish with the orange twist, expressing its oil onto the surface, rubbing it onto the rim of the glass, and dropping it in, peel side up. *Makes 1*

WINTER SQUASH

A Winter Squash cocktail is somewhat unexpected. This comes from Phoebe Wilson, co-owner of The Dogwood Cocktail Cabin in Crested Butte, Colorado. I love her culinary take on cocktails. Winter spices and warm roasted butternut squash are infused into vodka, creating a drink with deep, earthy sugar and spice flavors.

1 small butternut squash (about 1 pound)
1 (750 ml) bottle vodka
2 tbsp / 1 fl oz simple syrup (see page 6)
1 tbsp / ½ fl oz freshly squeezed lemon juice
1 tbsp / ½ fl oz freshly squeezed lime juice
1 sage leaf, as garnish
1 big pinch ground cinnamon, as garnish
1 big pinch freshly grated nutmeg, as garnish

Make the infusion: Place the oven rack in the center position and preheat the oven to 450°F. Place the whole butternut squash on a baking sheet and bake until blistered and soft enough that you can easily pierce the skin with a knife, about 1½ hours. Remove from the oven and set aside until cool enough to handle but still quite warm.

Cut the squash in half lengthwise and scoop out the seeds and fibers from the center. Pull off the skin and cut the flesh into 2-inch chunks. Place the pieces in a large, nonreactive container or Mason jar. Add the vodka while the squash is still warm; this will help the infusion process. Cover and set aside in a dark area for 5 days, swirling the mixture occasionally.

Taste the infusion; it should have a pronounced sweet squash flavor and be amber in color. If so, strain the liquid through a wire-mesh sieve lined with a double layer of damp cheesecloth, discarding the solids. This infusion makes more than you need for just one cocktail, but it can be covered and refrigerated for up to 1 month.

Make the cocktail: In a cocktail shaker ⅔ filled with medium ice cubes, combine ½ cup of the butternut-infused vodka with the simple syrup, lemon juice, and lime juice. Shake vigorously until well chilled. Strain into a chilled 6-ounce cocktail or martini glass. Float a sage leaf on top. Mix together the cinnamon and nutmeg, and sprinkle lightly on top. *Makes 1*

SCANDI GIBSON

Have I mentioned that I love Bittermens Orchard Street Celery Shrub? It shows its particular genius with anything aquavit. In this case, Avery Glasser from Bittermens takes it one glorious step further by reimagining the Gibson with their Hellfire Habanero Shrub added. I don't know why they left out the word "damnation." I guess it's implied. But hellfire *damnation* if this isn't one fine drink.

2 pony shots / 60 ml / 2 fl oz aquavit
1 pony shot / 30 ml / 1 fl oz Cocchi Americano
10 drops Bittermens Hellfire Habanero Shrub (available online)
20 drops Bittermens Orchard Street Celery Shrub (available online)
1 cocktail onion, as garnish

Combine the aquavit, Cocchi, and both shrubs in a mixing glass half-filled with ice. Stir until chilled and properly diluted, about 20 seconds. Julep-strain into a chilled old-fashioned or coupe glass. Garnish with a cocktail onion.   *Makes 1*

THE SPICE TRAIL

This drink is the result of my recent discovery of Bittermens Xocolatl Mole Bitters. It may seem unpronounceable (*so-co-laht*), but it's also unforgettable. They recommend it with dark rum, but I also like it with rye, as in this spicy update of a classic manhattan.

1 pony shot/ 60 ml / 2 fl oz rye
1 pony shot / 30 ml / 1 oz dry gin
1 tbsp / ½ fl oz St. Elizabeth Allspice Dram
1 tbsp / ½ fl oz red vermouth
2 dashes mole bitters, preferably Bittermens Xocolatl Mole Bitters
    (available online, optional)
1 barspoon clove-infused honey syrup (see page 8)
1 cocktail cherry, preferably Luxardo, as garnish

Combine the rye, gin, allspice dram, vermouth, and bitters (if using) in a mixing glass half-filled with ice. Scoop the honey syrup onto a barspoon and stir it in until the drink is well chilled and properly diluted and the syrup is completely incorporated, about 20 seconds. Julep-strain into a chilled coupe glass. Garnish with the cherry.   *Makes 1*

RUM-MUDDLED DIPLOMAT

I love the image of a Rum-Muddled Diplomat: an older gentlemen, dressed to the hilt in some muggy, tropical locale. He's a little daft and a little too self-important, sure. Of course he loves his rum, and of course he's beloved by everyone.

½ lime, quartered

1 pinch kosher salt

1 (1-inch) piece unpeeled English cucumber, quartered

2 pony shots / 60 ml / 2 fl oz añejo rum

1 scant barspoon habanero agave syrup, or to taste (see page 8)

2 dashes Bittercube Jamaican #1 Bitters (available online, optional)

1 splash club soda

1 very thin slice cucumber, as garnish

In a sturdy, thick-bottomed pint glass from a Boston shaker, use a bar muddler to crush the lime and salt until most of the lime juice is extracted. Add the quartered cucumber and continue to muddle until you have a fragrant, pulpy mush; it's okay if the lime and cucumber skins are still partly intact. Pour in the rum and spoon the habanero agave syrup onto the mixture; stir lightly to combine and to remove all the syrup from the spoon. Add the bitters (if using).

Fill the metal part of the Boston shaker ⅔ full with ice. Pour the muddled rum mixture (including pulp) over the ice and then cap the shaker with the pint glass. Shake vigorously until well chilled. Uncap the pint glass and add the club soda. Using a Hawthorn strainer, double-strain the cocktail through a wire-mesh sieve into a chilled cocktail glass. Float the cucumber slice on top. *Makes 1*

COOL AND STARRY

When you're in the mood for travel, consider this spiced rum and ginger beer cooler. It's lighter and less sweet than its classic predecessor, the Dark and Stormy—although either will cool you down when you're hot.

1 shot / 45 ml / 1½ fl oz spiced rum

¾ cup / 6 fl oz ginger beer

1 whole star anise, as garnish

Fill a large Collins or chimney glass with medium ice cubes. Pour in the rum and ginger beer and stir gently. Garnish with the star anise. *Makes 1*

BURNING SENSATION

That burning sensation you feel is my version of a "hopped-up" Tequila Sour.

2 pony shots / 60 ml / 2 fl oz tequila reposado
½ shot / 22½ ml / ¾ fl oz freshly squeezed lemon juice
¼ pony shot / 7½ ml / ¼ fl oz habanero agave syrup (see page 8)
1 small egg white (optional)
2 dashes Bittermens Hopped Grapefruit Bitters (available online, optional)

Pour the tequila, lemon juice, agave syrup, egg white (if using), and bitters (if using) into a cocktail shaker. Cover and vigorously "dry shake" the ingredients for about 30 seconds to combine. Don't skip this step—it really helps build structure. In fact, the longer and more vigorously you shake, the more lift you'll get from the foam that's created. Uncap the shaker and fill ⅔ full with medium ice cubes, then shake vigorously again until frothy, at least 30 seconds. Using a Hawthorn strainer, double-strain the cocktail through a wire-mesh sieve into a chilled coupe or cocktail glass. Wait a moment for the foam to rise, then serve. *Makes 1*

THAI BIRD CHILE KAMIKAZE

This concoction is made in the style of beverages bearing the name of Japanese pilots who carried out suicide attacks during World War II. Kamikazes typically consist of vodka, lime juice, and something sweet, and I've followed that basic outline here. This one is smoking hot, though, with the addition of a type of chile known as Thai bird. Make the vodka infusion as hot as you dare.

1 shot / 45 ml / 1½ fl oz Thai bird chile–infused vodka (see page 12)
1½ tbsp / ¾ fl oz freshly squeezed lime juice
1½ tbsp / ¾ fl oz herbal lemon syrup, made with cilantro (see page 7)
1 lime wheel, as garnish

Pour the infused vodka, lime juice, and herbal lemon syrup into a cocktail shaker half-filled with cracked ice; cover and shake vigorously. Strain into a chilled highball or cocktail glass. Garnish with the lime slice. *Makes 1*

WARM CARDIGAN

Hot drinks seem to have medicinal value. When winter rolls around, I consider these warm libations to be the original "nighttime sniffling sneezing coughing aching stuffy head fever" medicine. Of course, I don't know how much actual medical science is behind that theory, but the Warm Cardigan or Pink Peppercorn Hot Gin Sling might make even the flu seem fun.

½ cup / 4 fl oz strong, hot chamomile tea
2 pony shots / 60 ml / 2 fl oz genever, preferably Bols
2 cardamom pods
1 barspoon clove-infused honey syrup (see page 8)
1 dash Scrappy's Lavender Bitters (available online, optional)
1 thinly sliced lemon wheel, as garnish

Stir the tea and gin together in a heatproof mug or glass. Pinch the cardamom pods to crush them slightly and then drop them into the hot drink; stir in the honey syrup and bitters (if using). Garnish with the lemon. Let the flavors come together for about 3 minutes, then serve warm. *Makes 1*

PINK PEPPERCORN HOT GIN SLING

The Sling is one of the oldest styles of drinks, and these days you'll see all sorts of cocktails bearing this moniker. Historically, however, "cocktails" contained vermouth or bitters for medicinal purposes, so Slings wouldn't have been considered cocktails because they contained neither. My hot version stays very true to the original intention of a Sling, but I still consider it a cocktail. The aromatic addition of pink peppercorns makes it just modern enough for me.

1 sugar cube
½ cup / 4 fl oz boiling water
1½ tbsp / ¾ fl oz freshly squeezed lemon juice
2 pony shots / 60 ml / 2 fl oz dry gin
8 or 10 pink peppercorns

Place the sugar cube in the bottom of a heatproof mug or glass; pour in the boiling water. Add the lemon juice and gin. Stir gently, but don't bother to dissolve the sugar cube completely. Pinch the pink peppercorns to slightly crush them and then drop them into the drink. Let the flavors come together for 3 minutes. Serve warm. *Makes 1*

HOLLAND RAZOR BLADE

This is a cocktail that's uniquely off-kilter, a lot like Amsterdam itself. Sure, the city sparkles like the canals that run through it, but it's also got an unexpected edge: hot and sweet at the same time. At first glance Amsterdam seems like a rather traditional, tightly built European capital. Its buildings stack up like slender dominoes topped by ornate gables. But look again and you might notice the way the buildings along the canals seem to lean awkwardly toward the water. This isn't due to age or shoddy workmanship, nor is it from the genever they offered you at lunch. These quirky angles were designed to assist in the hauling of cargo into the warehouses above. Surprisingly ingenious. I adapted this recipe from *Around the World with Jigger, Beaker, and Flask* by Charles Henry Baker, Jr. (1939), because it seems like a perfect marriage of spirit and recipe.

> 2 pony shots / 60 ml / 2 fl oz genever
> 1 tbsp / ½ fl oz freshly squeezed lemon juice
> 1 tbsp / ½ fl oz simple syrup (see page 6)
> 1 pinch cayenne pepper

Add the gin, lemon juice, and simple syrup to a cocktail shaker ⅔ filled with medium ice cubes. Shake vigorously until well chilled. Strain into a chilled coupe or cocktail glass; sprinkle with cayenne. *Makes 1*

Gin, Gin, Gin, or Genever?

Genever is considered the original gin. It's often called Dutch gin, but it's not really gin, though it's made with a botanically infused neutral spirit. If you were to mix a martini with it, you'd take one sip and wonder what kind of funky gin you were drinking. That's because its base spirit is malt wine (but don't get too hung up on "wine").

Old Tom Gin is the missing link and may have come about as a steppingstone between genever and what we know as gin today.

London Dry Gin is the gin we know as gin. It's what you'll want in that G&T or martini I mentioned. It's produced just about anywhere in the world. Distillers have room to play with the botanicals, meaning that many gins have their own distinctive flavors, but the defining component is always juniper.

Plymouth Dry Gin is a brand, yes. But it's also the only gin that carries its own Designation of Origin—meaning that European law mandates it can only be made in Plymouth, England.

HERBAL

Farm to table. Field to plate. Why not garden to glass? Herbal cocktails have a botanical bite that defines them. Mint. Basil. Cilantro. Sage. Rosemary. Dill. These herbs, as fresh as the season, can be muddled, infused, and steeped into syrups and shrubs, or simply snipped and stuck on top. There's an herb for every season and every palate. I even have a cocktail section in my garden.

TRIPLE C COLLINS

When you're out in the garden gathering your cocktail ingredients, there's no reason to stop at herbs. This Triple C Collins (the C stands for celery, cucumber, and cilantro) brings all sorts of garden bounty to the glass.

1 lemon wedge, for moistening and as garnish

Celery salt, for rimming the glass

1 pinch kosher salt

1 (1½-inch) piece unpeeled English cucumber, roughly chopped, about ¼ cup

2 small, light-colored interior celery stalks with leaves, divided

¼ cup loosely packed fresh cilantro

2 shots / 90 ml / 3 fl oz cucumber-infused vodka
  (see Mild-Flavored Vegetable Infusion on page 12)

2 tbsp / 1 fl oz freshly squeezed lemon juice

2 or 3 dashes celery bitters

¼ cup / 2 fl oz club soda, or as needed

1 spear unpeeled English cucumber, as garnish

Use the lemon wedge to lightly moisten the rim of a 10 to 14-ounce Collins glass. Pour celery salt into a small saucer, spreading it out in a thin, even layer. Press the glass rim into the celery salt, cookie-cutter style, twisting it back and forth to coat the rim evenly.

Roughly chop one of the celery stalks; you should have about ¼ cup. In a sturdy, thick-bottomed pint glass from a Boston shaker, use a bar muddler to crush the kosher salt, chopped cucumber, chopped celery, and cilantro into a fragrant, pulpy mush. Add the vodka, lemon juice, and bitters; swirl to combine.

Fill the metal part of the Boston shaker half-full with ice. Pour the muddled vodka mixture (including pulp) over the ice. Cap the shaker with its pint glass and shake vigorously until well chilled. Using a Hawthorn strainer, double-strain the cocktail through a wire-mesh sieve into an ice-filled highball glass. Top with club soda and stir gently. Garnish with the remaining celery stalk, the cucumber spear, and the lemon wedge. *Makes 1*

BREEDER'S CUP

Breeder's Cup is from Matthew Biancaniello, the well-known cocktail chef at the Hollywood Roosevelt Hotel's Library Bar. His talents are evident here, as is his creative ability to reimagine the classic Gordon's Cup cocktail as a horserace, leading to his pungent addition of horseradish and a whole new breed of beverage.

6 (⅛-inch) English cucumber slices, divided
½ shot / 22½ ml / ¾ fl oz freshly squeezed lime juice
½ shot / 22½ ml / ¾ fl oz agave syrup*
1 barspoon beet horseradish
2 pony shots / 60 ml / 2 fl oz dry gin
1 pinch smoked sea salt, as garnish

Mix agave nectar and water in a 1:1 ratio.

Line the sides of an old-fashioned glass with 3 slices of the cucumber in an attractive pattern. Fill the glass with medium ice cubes. In a sturdy, thick-bottomed pint glass from a Boston shaker, use a bar muddler to crush the remaining cucumber slices with the lime juice and agave syrup until fragrant. Add the beet horseradish and gin, stirring to combine and to remove all the horseradish from the spoon.

Fill the metal part of the Boston shaker ⅔ full with ice. Pour the muddled gin mixture (including pulp) over the ice. Cap the shaker with the pint glass and shake vigorously until well chilled. Using a Hawthorn strainer, double-strain the cocktail through a wire-mesh sieve into the prepared glass. Garnish with a pinch of smoked sea salt. *Makes 1*

TOM AND DAISY

A "Daisy" is an old style of cocktail; its base spirit and fruity element are changeable, but a Daisy is always served over crushed ice.

2½ pony shots / 75 ml / 2½ fl oz Ransom or other Old Tom gin
1 shot / 30 ml / 1 fl oz freshly squeezed lemon juice
½ pony shot / 15 ml / ½ fl oz yellow Chartreuse
Splash of club soda
1 fresh mint sprig, as garnish

Add the gin, lemon juice, and Chartreuse to a cocktail shaker ⅔ filled with ice. Cover and shake vigorously. Strain into an 8 to 10-ounce highball glass filled with crushed ice. Top with club soda and garnish with mint. *Makes 1*

BEETLE JUICE

I somehow got it into my head that I needed to "invent" a cocktail using the strangest ingredient I could think of, so I chose beets and came up with Beetle Juice. But do you know what? Beet cocktails aren't so strange; in fact, they're quite trendy. Just go online if you don't believe me. Since I like pickled beets, I turned my attention to a cocktail featuring a beet and juniper berry shrub.

2 pony shots / 60 ml / 2 fl oz beet-infused dry gin or vodka, as you prefer
   (see page 12)
2 tbsp / 1 fl oz beet and juniper berry shrub (see page 11)
1 tbsp / ½ fl oz freshly squeezed lemon juice
¼ to ⅜ cup / 2 to 3 fl oz tonic water
1 pickled beet from the shrub preparation, as garnish (see page 11)
1 trimmed scallion, as garnish
Coarse salt and freshly cracked pepper, to taste

Fill an 8 to 10-ounce wine goblet or highball glass with medium ice cubes; add the beet-infused liquor, shrub, and lemon juice. Gently stir until just blended. Top with tonic water and stir gently. Garnish with a pickled beet and scallion and season with a tiny pinch each of salt and pepper. *Makes 1*

A SAVORY COCKTAIL

Part of the fun in writing this book was asking people what a "savory cocktail" meant to them. I got all kinds of answers. One of the people I asked was Andy Windak, one of my podcast partners at *The Table Set*. His answer was so smart and succinct, I couldn't believe I hadn't thought of it myself.

1 shot / 45 ml / 1½ fl oz savory-infused dry gin (see Herbal Infusion page 12)*

2 tbsp / 1 fl oz freshly squeezed lemon juice

½ pony shot / 15 ml / ½ fl oz red vermouth

1 small egg white (optional)

1 small savory sprig, as garnish (optional)*

* Savory (Satureja hortensis and Satureja montana) are culinary herbs in the mint family. Any fragrant herb may be substituted.

Pour the gin, lemon juice, vermouth, and egg white (if using) into cocktail shaker. Cover and vigorously "dry shake" for about 30 seconds to combine. Uncap the shaker, fill ⅔ full with ice, and shake vigorously again until frothy, at least 30 seconds. Using a Hawthorn strainer, double-strain the cocktail through a wire-mesh sieve into a chilled coupe glass. Garnish with the sprig of savory (if using). *Makes 1*

CELERY SHRUB COCKTAIL

I chose aquavit for this Celery Shrub Cocktail. It's the Scandinavian cousin to vodka. But unlike *Patty Duke's* Patty and Cathy, they're hardly identical cousins. Aquavit is distinctly flavored with caraway seed. As a chilled shot in a stemmed glass it's the perfect partner to savory foods. These same characteristics lend themselves to savory cocktails. I like an American version called Krogstad from House Spirits Distillery in Portland, Oregon, with a recipe based on the traditional Scandinavian method for its clear, clean taste.

2 pony shots / 60 ml / 2 fl oz aquavit

½ pony shot / 15 ml / ½ fl oz Cardamaro or other herbaceous amaro

½ pony shot / 15 ml / ½ fl oz Bittermens Orchard Street Celery Shrub (available online)

1 lemon twist, as garnish

Combine the aquavit, Cardamaro, and celery shrub in a mixing glass half-filled with ice. Stir until chilled and properly diluted, about 20 seconds. Julep-strain into a chilled coupe or cocktail glass. Garnish with a lemon twist, expressing its oil onto the surface, rubbing it onto the rim of the glass, and dropping it in the drink, peel side up. *Makes 1*

PIMM'S CUP UP

I love to take walks in the summertime. I live in Los Angeles, where we're drowning in sunshine—yet it's rarely too sweltering to enjoy a stroll. The city has a different beat in summer. Cafés spill out onto the street and menus get written up on chalkboards. Summer cocktails whisper their minty cool breath in my ear. On one such afternoon, I wandered into a little place on Beverly Boulevard. The board was chalked with the phrase, "Beat the heat with a cool cocktail: Pimm's Cup." I'd never had the drink, so I sat down and said "Pimm's Cup, please, *up*." Well, the waiter's bemused face made me appreciate the phrase "walking in LA." Because nobody walks in LA, except fools like me.

3 thin, wide ribbons of English cucumber peel, cut lengthwise with
    a vegetable peeler from a 3-inch section
1 (1-inch) piece English cucumber, roughly chopped
3 dime-size slices fresh ginger
9 mint leaves, divided
1 tiny pinch sea salt
1 shot / 45 ml / 1½ fl oz Pimm's No.1
1 shot / 45 ml / 1½ fl oz dry gin
½ pony shot / 15 ml / ½ fl oz ginger liqueur
½ pony shot / 15 ml / ½ fl oz freshly squeezed lemon juice

Line the inside of a cocktail glass with the cucumber ribbons. They should easily stick to the glass; if not, moisten them with a little water. Set aside.

In a sturdy, thick-bottomed pint glass from a Boston shaker, use a bar muddler to crush the cucumber piece, ginger, 8 mint leaves, and salt into a fragrant, pulpy mush. Pour in the Pimm's, gin, ginger liqueur, and lemon juice.

Fill the metal part of the Boston shaker ⅔ full with medium ice cubes. Pour the muddled Pimm's mixture (including pulp) over the ice. Cap the shaker with the pint glass and shake vigorously until well chilled. Using a Hawthorn strainer, double-strain the cocktail through a wire-mesh sieve into the prepared glass. Garnish with remaining mint leaf. *Makes 1*

Tip

For a simpler version, you can forget the ribbons and the muddle of cucumber, ginger, and mint. Build the drink in an ice-filled highball glass, topping it with 2 to 3 ounces of San Pellegrino Limonata or club soda, then garnish with a cucumber spear and mint leaves. This is a more traditional variation on the Pimm's Cup. It will lose some of its savory edge but will remain a refreshing summer cocktail.

GREENS FEE FIZZ

I don't golf, but I've been to the proverbial 19th hole a time or two. I always notice that many people are drinking plain old gin and tonic, and it got me wondering. Can you make a gin fizz with tonic water instead of soda water? Well, let's find out.

2 pony shots / 60 ml / 2 fl oz dry gin
½ pony shot / 15 ml / ½ fl oz green Chartreuse
1 tbsp / ½ fl oz freshly squeezed lime juice
1 barspoon herbal lemon syrup, using mixed herbs (see page 7)
3 or 4 drops celery bitters (optional)
¼ cup / 2 fl oz tonic water
1 celery stalk, as garnish

Combine the gin, Chartreuse, lime juice, herbal syrup, bitters (if using), and tonic water in a cocktail shaker half-filled with ice. Cover and shake vigorously until well chilled; strain into an ice-filled Collins or chimney glass. Garnish with the celery stalk. *Makes 1*

TO HELL WITH SPAIN #2

This drink is from Bittercube's cocktail bitters Ira Koplowitz. Its dual notes of cocoa and rhubarb round out the distinctive herbal notes in the dill-infused aquavit.

¼ pony shot / 7½ ml / ¼ fl oz green Chartreuse, as rinse
1 pony shot / 30 ml / 1 fl oz dill-infused aquavit (see Herbal Infusion, page 12)
1 pony shot / 30 ml / 1 fl oz Cocchi Vermouth di Torino, or other red vermouth
¼ pony shot / 7½ ml / ¼ fl oz cherry liqueur
1½ tsp / ¼ fl oz freshly squeezed lemon juice
¾ tsp / ⅛ fl oz simple syrup (see page 6)
1 dash Bittercube blackstrap molasses bitters (available online)

Pour the Chartreuse into a chilled cocktail glass and "turn" the glass, rolling the Chartreuse along the inside until is well coated; pour out the excess. This is called "rinsing" the glass. Set aside.

Add the aquavit, vermouth, cherry liqueur, lemon juice, simple syrup, and bitters to a mixing glass half-filled with ice. Stir until chilled and properly diluted, about 20 seconds. Strain into the prepared glass. *Makes 1*

GOLDEN LION

The Golden Lion is from lead bartender Jacob Grier from Metrovino in Portland, Oregon. The cumin notes in his cocktail come from an American version of aquavit made at North Shore Distillery.

1 shot / 45 ml / 1½ fl oz white vermouth
½ shot / 22½ ml / ¾ fl oz aquavit
½ pony shot / 15 ml / ½ fl oz Galliano L'Autentico
2 dashes celery bitters

Combine the vermouth, aquavit, Galliano, and bitters in a mixing glass half-filled with ice. Stir until chilled and properly diluted, about 20 seconds. Julep-strain into a chilled coupe or cocktail glass. Serve immediately. *Makes 1*

FENNEL FIZZ

Fennel has a natural "fizz" that makes the tongue tingle. That tingle comes from anise and its menthol undertones. This is psychological, but it opens the palate for the subtle flavors that fennel has to offer. The savory notes in sage keep this cocktail in balance.

1 (2-inch) piece fennel, sliced (stalk only)
4 large sage leaves
1 pinch coarse salt
2 pony shots / 60 ml / 2 fl oz citrus-infused vodka (see page 12), or dry gin if you prefer
½ pony / 15 ml / ½ fl oz green Chartreuse
2 tbsp / 1 fl oz freshly squeezed lemon juice
1 barspoon herbal lemon syrup, made with mixed herbs (see page 7)
⅜ cup / 3 fl oz club soda, or more as needed
1 fennel frond, as garnish

In a sturdy, thick-bottomed pint glass from a Boston shaker, use a bar muddler to crush together the fennel slices, sage, and salt until you have a fragrant, pulpy mush. Add the vodka or gin, Chartreuse, lemon juice, and herbal lemon syrup; stir lightly to combine and to remove all the syrup from the spoon.

Fill the metal part of the Boston shaker ⅔ full with medium ice cubes. Pour the muddled gin or vodka mixture (including pulp) over the ice. Cap the shaker with the pint glass and shake vigorously until well chilled. Using a Hawthorn strainer, double-strain the cocktail through a wire-mesh sieve into an ice-filled highball glass. Top with club soda and stir gently. Garnish with the fennel frond. *Makes 1*

SALAD BOWL GIN AND TONIC

This drink feels like summer. Make it with the very best summer tomatoes or don't make it at all. Backyard beauties are best, but farmers' markets and even some grocery stores carry excellent heirloom tomatoes these days. Choose carefully; you'll want a bright tomato taste to stand up to the fearless herbaceousness in this cocktail, which drinks like a meal.

¼ cup loosely packed fresh herbs (such as parsley, thyme, basil, and tarragon leaves)
¼ cup roughly chopped heirloom tomato
1 (1-inch) piece unpeeled English cucumber, roughly chopped (about ¼ cup)
2 pony shots / 60 ml / 2 fl oz dry gin
Tonic water, as needed
2 sprigs parsley, basil, or other herb, as garnish (optional)

Choose a traditional pint or similar sturdy, thick-bottomed 16-ounce glass. If any of the herbs (such as thyme) have woody stems, remove and discard them. Place the herbs, tomato, and cucumber in the glass and use a long-handled bar muddler to crush them into a fragrant, pulpy mush. Fill the glass with medium ice cubes, stir, add the gin, and stir again. Top with tonic water. Garnish with the herb sprigs (if using). *Makes 1*

SCARBOROUGH FAIR

Are you going? I think you should.

¼ cup / 2 fl oz vodka infused with equal parts parsley, sage, rosemary, and thyme
    (see page 12)
½ pony shot / 15ml / ½ fl oz white vermouth
½ pony shot / 15ml / ½ fl oz freshly squeezed lemon juice
1½ tsp / ¼ fl oz citrus syrup, made with lemon (see page 8)
1 small fresh thyme sprig, as garnish

Combine the vodka, vermouth, lemon juice, and citrus syrup in a cocktail shaker ⅔ full of ice. Cover and shake vigorously until well chilled, then strain into a chilled coupe or cocktail glass. Garnish with the thyme sprig. *Makes 1*

THE GRAZER'S EDGE

This is a summery drink, but that doesn't mean you have to wait for summer to enjoy it. This is another cocktail that I prefer to make by the pitcherful, or sometimes the jarful. Large Mason jars are a great addition to the home bartender's supply closet. They're great for making infusions because they come with easy-on, easy-off screw lids. Since this is a party drink, I think it's fun to use smaller Mason or jelly jars as glasses. It makes casual entertaining seem all the more lighthearted.

3 limes, divided
½ cup packed fresh basil sprigs, plus more as garnish
1 unpeeled English cucumber
2 tbsp / 1 fl oz herbal lemon syrup, using basil (see page 7)
1½ cups / 12 fl oz citrus or cucumber-infused vodka (see page 12)
½ cup / 4 fl oz Cocchi Americano
3 cups / 24 fl oz club soda, or as needed

Slice 1 lime into thin rounds and place them into a 2-pint or larger pitcher or Mason jar. Juice the remaining limes and add the juice to the pitcher or jar. Slice the cucumber in half crosswise; cut half into thin rounds, the other half into 6 lengthwise spears. Add the rounds to the jar or pitcher; reserve the spears to use as garnish.

Add the vodka, Cocchi, and ½ cup basil to the pitcher or jar. Cover and place in the refrigerator to steep for at least 30 minutes, or up to 8 hours.

Fill 6 Collins glasses, double old-fashioned glasses, or 12-ounce Mason jars with medium ice cubes. Strain the mixture from the jar or pitcher, dividing it equally among the glasses (about ⅜ cup / 3 fl oz each). Top each with club soda (⅜ to ½ cup / 3 to 4 fl oz) and garnish with a basil sprig and cucumber spear. Serve with a straw. *Makes 6*

THIS FEELING OF JOY

In some Southeast Asian cultures, lemongrass is thought to have powers of psychic purification. I chose Żubrówka vodka to carry on the theme of grass in this cocktail, which is essentially a lemongrass sour. Originating in the 17th century, this very dry style of vodka is flavored with a tincture of European buffalo grass. A single blade is traditionally placed inside each bottle as well. This infusion gives the liquor a faint greenish yellow tint and the delicate herbal aroma of freshly mown grass.

1 (2-inch) piece fresh lemongrass, split into quarters lengthwise
2 pony shots / 60 ml / 2 fl oz Żubrówka Vodka, or substitute citrus-infused vodka
    (see page 12)
1½ tbsp / ¾ fl oz freshly squeezed lime juice
1½ tsp / ¼ fl oz lemongrass kaffir syrup (see page 7)
1 small egg white (optional)
3 drops Angostura bitters, or Aromatic "House" Bitters (see page 10, optional)
3 drops The Bitter End Thai Bitters (available online, optional)

In a sturdy, thick-bottomed cocktail shaker, use a bar muddler to crush the lemongrass until fragrant. Pour the vodka, lime juice, lemongrass kaffir syrup, and egg white (if using). Cover and vigorously "dry shake" the ingredients for about 30 seconds to combine. Don't skip this step—it really helps build structure. The longer and more vigorously you shake, the more lift you'll get from the foam that's created. Uncap the shaker and fill ⅔ full with ice; shake vigorously until well chilled and frothy, at least 30 more seconds. Using a Hawthorn strainer, double-strain the cocktail through a wire-mesh sieve into a chilled coupe or cocktail glass. Wait a moment for the foam to rise, then place 3 drops of each kind of bitters (if using) to form a circle on top and use a skewer to connect the dots. *Makes 1*

UMAMI

Just what the heck is an umami cocktail—or umami in general, for that matter? We typically consider four basic flavors—sweet, salty, sour, and bitter—when we describe taste. But our taste receptors are also able to pick out a more nuanced flavor. The Japanese have a name for it, umami *(oo-MA-mee)*. This "fifth flavor" has lately become a hot topic in the culinary world.

The common denominator in umami flavors is a high concentration of certain amino acids. They make things taste more intense, more rounded, more complete. They satisfy the soul. Soy sauce, miso, anchovies, shellfish, toasted nuts, vinegar, and sautéed mushrooms are umami flavor boosters.

BLOODY MARY

The Bloody Mary became an instant classic upon its arrival in the mid 1930s. Then it was little more than tomato juice and vodka—a bit milder than the quintessential brunch drink of today. The modern, spiced-up version has become massively popular. Everyone has their own set of rules, complete with secret ingredients and "must-have" garnishes. This is one of my favorite variations.

2 pony shots / 60 ml / 2 fl oz vodka (or try black pepper or celery-infused vodka, see page 12)
½ cup / 4 fl oz Savory Tomato Juice (see page 67)
½ barspoon grated fresh horseradish, or more to taste
3 dashes Worcestershire sauce
2 dashes red Tabasco sauce, or more to taste
1 pinch kosher salt
1 pinch black pepper, or more to taste
Garnishes of choice, such as celery sticks, cherry peppers, citrus wedges, pickled okra, olives

Combine the vodka, tomato juice, horseradish, Worcestershire, Tabasco, salt, and pepper in a mixing glass. Using a second mixing glass, gently pour the ingredients back and forth between glasses until thoroughly mixed. Pour the cocktail into any large, ice-filled glass and garnish to taste. Serve with a straw for stirring and sipping. *Makes 1*

SUNGOLD ZINGER

This drink has made seasonal appearances on the menu at Range in San Francisco's Mission District for almost a decade. But don't think of this cocktail as another variation on the Bloody Mary—its charms are far more understated.

4 Sungold cherry tomatoes, halved*
1 pinch coarse salt
1 shot / 45 ml / 1½ fl oz dry gin
½ pony shot / 15 ml / ½ fl oz elderflower liqueur
1 tbsp / ½ fl oz freshly squeezed lemon juice
1 whole Sungold cherry tomato, as garnish*

Sweet cherry, grape, or yellow pear tomatoes can be substituted.

In a sturdy, thick-bottomed pint glass from a Boston shaker, use a bar muddler to crush the halved tomatoes with the salt until most of the juice is extracted and you have a fragrant, pulpy mush. Add the gin, elderflower liqueur, and lemon juice; swirl to combine.

Fill the metal part of the Boston shaker ⅔ full of ice. Pour the muddled gin mixture (including pulp) over the ice cubes, then cap the shaker with the pint glass. Shake vigorously until well chilled.

Using a Hawthorn strainer, double-strain the cocktail through a wire-mesh sieve into a chilled cocktail glass. Garnish with the whole tomato.   *Makes 1*

TARTUFO

This cocktail seems fresh and light at first glance, but behind all those bubbles and bright botanicals there's a dark earthiness. It comes from truffle-infused honey, available in most good cheese shops, at gourmet markets, and online.

2 pony shots / 60 ml / 2 fl oz dry gin
2 tbsp / 1 fl oz freshly squeezed lemon juice
1 tbsp / ½ fl oz truffle honey syrup*
2 fresh rosemary sprigs, divided
¼ to ⅜ cup / 2 to 3 fl oz club soda

Combine black truffle honey and warm water in a 1:2 ratio.

Stir together the gin, lemon juice, and honey syrup in a cocktail shaker, making sure the honey dissolves completely. Slap 1 rosemary sprig between both of your hands, or gently pinch it all over to release the oils, and add to the shaker. Fill the shaker ⅔ full with ice; cap and shake vigorously until the cocktail is well chilled. Using a Hawthorn strainer, double-strain through a wire-mesh sieve into an ice-filled highball glass. Top with club soda and stir gently. Garnish with the remaining rosemary sprig. *Makes 1*

TRUFFLE-INFUSED COGNAC

This isn't a cocktail per se, but it's so good it deserves a place of its own in this book. Sip it neat or on the rocks, or use it to replace the whiskey or brandy in an old-fashioned for a very savory take on that classic. This is a specialty of Canon: Whiskey and Bitters Emporium in Seattle.

1 (750 ml) bottle cognac
1 or 2 (1½ inch) black truffles, sliced, to taste

Pour the cognac in to a large jar and add the black truffles. Cover and let infuse for about 1 week. Working in batches, strain the liquor through a coffee filter to remove any particulates.

Don't confuse truffles with truffles. What I mean is that these cocktails aren't deep, dark chocolate sippers. The truffle I'm talking about is a type of subterranean mushroom—an elusive, warty black or white fungus found mostly in the regions of Périgord in France or Alba in Italy, respectively. Unattractive in appearance and named after the Latin for "lump," truffles impart an exquisite, pungent flavor when shaved over pasta or used in an egg dish. They're expensive and hard to find, so now you want them, right?

Silk and Gators is a smoothly elegant, deeply nuanced cognac cocktail—hence the "silk" in its title. But it's the complex earthiness of the "gator" that got my attention in this Paul Sanguinetti cocktail from Ray's and Stark Bar at the Los Angeles County Museum of Art. Nutty, leathery, salty, bitter, toffee, and savory—all at the same time. I was first introduced to Paul's cocktails at a press event, and I immediately noticed that several creations on his list featured some sort of wine element. It turns out that he has a sommelier background, making his cocktail menus some of the more surprising I've seen in a long time.

¼ pony shot / 7½ ml / ¼ fl oz Calisaya amaro or other herbaceous amaro or liqueur, as rinse

2 pony shots / 60 ml / 2 fl oz cognac

½ shot / 22½ ml / ¾ fl oz sherry (Apostoles 30 Year Palo Cortado is preferred, if you can find it)

½ pony shot / 15 ml / ½ fl oz red vermouth

1 large, wide orange peel chip, as garnish

Pour the amaro or liqueur into a chilled coupe or cocktail glass and swirl the glass, rolling the liquid until the inside is well coated; pour out the excess. This is known as rinsing the glass. Set aside.

Add the cognac, sherry, and vermouth to a mixing glass half-filled with ice. Stir until chilled and properly diluted, about 20 seconds. Strain into the prepared glass. Garnish with the orange chip, expressing its oil onto the surface, rubbing it onto the glass rim, and dropping it in, peel side up. *Makes 1*

No longer designated as solely a libation for stereotypical dowagers and spinsters, sherry is gaining well-deserved recognition as a complex, interesting, and food-friendly alternative to traditional wines and cocktails. Sherry gets its name from an anglicization of the word *Jerez (Xerex)*, which refers to the area of southern Spain where sherry is produced. Made using a network of barrels known as *soleras*, old and new wines are fractionally blended to ensure consistency.

Sherry comes in many styles, ranging from dry and pale to quite dark and unctuously sweet. The driest and palest type—called *Fino*—is light and crisp with a subtle brininess; it pairs extremely well with almonds, cheese, fried foods, olives, and seafood. Oloroso style is darker, fuller, and sometimes moderately sweet, and it can be paired with pungent cheeses, fatty meats, and nuts. *Palo Cortado* sherries possess both Fino and Oloroso characteristics, with complexities reminiscent of a fine cognac.

DOG'S NOSE

The Dog's Nose is mentioned in Charles Dickens's *The Pickwick Papers*. A character named Walker blames the drink for the crippling of his hand—not exactly a ringing endorsement. But I doubt that either Mr. Walker or Mr. Dickens imagined the umami boost that comes from a pinch of porcini powder.

> 2 shots / 90 ml / 3 fl oz dry gin
> 1 cup / 8 fl oz traditional-style porter, at room temperature*
> 1 tiny pinch porcini mushroom powder (directions below) or crystalline MSG powder
> Freshly grated nutmeg, as garnish
>
> *If you can't find porter, choose an Irish stout such as Guinness.*

Make the porcini mushroom powder: Place 1 cup dried porcini mushrooms (about 1 ounce) in a food processor. Pulse 10 or 12 times to break up the pieces, then process for at least 3 minutes until very finely ground. Store indefinitely in a dry place, covered. Makes about ¼ cup powder.

Make the cocktail: Pour the gin into a 10 to 14-ounce glass. Add the porter and allow the head to develop somewhat, then sprinkle on the mushroom powder. Garnish with nutmeg. *Makes 1*

BULLSHOT

The boldness of this drink comes from beef. To keep it from tasting like watery broth, I take the time to prepare a simple bouillon with a healthy dose of celery and black pepper. Avoid using the cubes from the grocery store—the result will be too salty.

> 4 cups / 1 quart high-quality low-sodium beef broth or homemade bouillon
> 2 pony shots / 60 ml / 2 fl oz vodka (or try black peppercorn or celery-infused vodka, see page 12)
> ½ pony shot / 15 ml / ½ fl oz freshly squeezed lemon juice
> 2 or 3 dashes celery bitters
> 1 or 2 dashes Worcestershire sauce
> 1 or 2 dashes red Tabasco sauce
> 1 lemon wedge, as garnish

To a cocktail shaker half-filled with medium ice cubes, add ½ cup chilled bouillon, vodka, lemon juice, bitters, Worcestershire, and Tabasco. Cover and shake vigorously, then strain into an ice-filled highball glass. Squeeze the lemon wedge over the drink and then drop it in. *Makes 1*

BLACK PEPPER OYSTER SHOOTERS

Long on umami, oyster shooters are a protein-packed favorite of the morning-after crowd. These briny beauties can be as simple as a few dashes of hot sauce splashed on the half shell and chased with cheap beer, good and cold. But there are other, more sophisticated approaches as well. My version retains all the expected flavors, allowing for the full umami effect. But in this case the booze isn't a vehicle to get that briny bivalve up and over the gag reflex. It's a boldly infused black pepper vodka that adds another layer of flavor. So quaff away. For you oyster neophytes, no chewing is necessary.

1½ cups Savory Tomato juice (see page 67)
24 fresh oysters
3 cups / 750 ml black pepper–infused vodka (see page 12)
Fresh horseradish root, peeled, to taste
Lemon wedges, to taste

Working one shooter at a time, spoon 1 tablespoon tomato juice into the bottom of a standard-size "double" shot glass (about 3-ounce size). Shuck an oyster and add it to the shot glass with all its liquor. Add 2 tablespoons (1 fl oz) infused vodka by pouring it gently over the back of a spoon to "float" it on top of the tomato juice. Finish with a grating of horseradish. Serve with lemon wedges on the side. *Makes 24*

Tip
Alternatively, you can serve this cocktail with black peppercorn–infused silver tequila (see page 12) and replace the horseradish with a thin slice of jalapeño.

PORK AND BEANS

Pork and Beans say umami to me, especially when they're made with bacon. Jeremy Schwartz and Taylor Brittenham ("Ms." and "His" to their patrons at pop-up bars around Los Angeles) are behind this creative cocktail. They're also the duo behind Bitter Tears Cocktail Bitters.

2 pony shots / 60 ml / 2 fl oz bourbon
½ shot / 22½ ml / ¾ fl oz coffee liqueur
3 or 4 dashes Bitter Tears "Ms. Piggy" Peppercorn Bacon Bitters (available online)

Combine the bourbon, coffee liqueur, and bitters in a mixing glass half-filled with ice. Gently stir until chilled and properly diluted, about 20 seconds. Julep-strain into a chilled coupe or cocktail glass. *Makes 1*

PICKLEBACK (MAKE MINE A DOUBLE)

The Pickleback. No one seems to want to claim this drink as their own, though its genesis appears to be in Brooklyn, New York. For a drink that nobody likes, it's awfully popular. Such a simple combination: 1 shot Jameson whiskey and 1 shot pickle brine—served in two glasses. You could just open a jar of Vlassics—I'm sure that's how it's usually done—but I prefer to tackle this cocktail with more culinary acumen.

2 pony shots / 60 ml / 2 fl oz whiskey (preferably Jameson)
2 pony shots / 60 ml / 2 fl oz Spicy Dill Pickle Brine (recipe follows)
Pickles, as garnish
Fresh dill sprigs, as garnish

Pour the whiskey and brine into separate "double" shot glasses (about 3-ounce size). Garnish as you like—I suggest you go overboard. *Makes 1*

HOMEMADE SPICY DILL PICKLES AND BRINE

3 cups white vinegar
3 cups water
2 tbsp sea salt
3 bunches fresh dill, roughly chopped
6 small cloves peeled garlic
1 red Thai bird chile, thinly sliced
2 heaping tsp dill seeds
2 tsp prepared pickling spice
½ tsp mustard seeds
3 pounds very small Kirby cucumbers, about 3 inches long

Sterilize 6 pint-size jars and lids according to the manufacturer's instructions. Meanwhile, combine the vinegar, water, and salt in a nonreactive medium saucepan; bring to a boil over medium-high heat, then lower the heat to a simmer.

Remove the hot jars from the sterilizing pot. Divide the dill, garlic, chile slices, dill seeds, pickling spice, and mustard seeds among the jars. Divide the cucumbers into 6 groups then tightly pack them into the jars. Pour the hot vinegar-water mixture over the cucumbers to within ½ inch of the rim. Secure the jars with the sterilized lids and bands. Place the jars back in the sterilizer or pot of water and process by boiling for 15 minutes. Remove carefully with tongs. Let cool, then store in a dry place for at least 3 weeks before opening. *Makes 6 pint-sized jars*

BITTER

Back in our vulnerable past, we relied on our detection of bitterness to warn us that certain plants shouldn't be eaten because they are toxic. So what can explain the trend toward bitter in modern-day cocktails? Sales of bitter liqueurs such as Campari and Fernet-Branca are way, way up—especially among the fashionable crowd in large metropolitan areas. Is the stylish set bent on destroying themselves through the consumption of the very bitter roots we are predisposed to avoid? Are tragically hip hipsters really that tragic? Is this a cruel form of natural selection? Or is there a certain beauty to be found in the forbidden?

BITTER BEAUTY

There's a reason I called this cocktail Bitter *Beauty*.

1 pony shot / 60 ml / 1 fl oz Campari
1 pony shot / 60 ml / 1 fl oz dry gin
½ pony shot / 15 ml / ½ fl oz white vermouth
¼ pony shot / 7½ ml / ¼ fl oz Fernet-Branca
¼ pony shot / 7½ ml / ¼ fl oz Cynar or other herbaceous amaro
3 drops orange bitters
1 orange twist, as garnish

Combine the Campari, gin, vermouth, Fernet-Branca, Cynar, and bitters in a mixing glass half-filled with cracked ice. Stir until chilled and properly diluted, about 20 seconds. Julep-strain into a chilled coupe or cocktail glass. Garnish with an orange twist, expressing its oil onto the surface, rubbing it onto the rim, and dropping it in the drink, peel side up.   *Makes 1*

CHARENTES SHRUB

The Charentes Shrub is from David Delaney, a busy bartender in Boston. His creation won *Imbibe Magazine*'s Cover Cocktail contest. The Pineau des Charentes in the drink caught my attention, so I tracked him down. I love how creatively he combines diverse ingredients into a savory cocktail that defies expectations.

> 1 shot / 45 ml / 1½ fl oz rye
>
> ½ shot / 22½ ml / ¾ fl oz Earl Grey–infused Pineau des Charentes*
>
> 1 tbsp / ½ fl oz pineapple rosemary shrub (see page 10)
>
> 1 tbsp / ½ fl oz freshly squeezed lemon juice
>
> 2 dashes orange bitters
>
> ¼ cup / 2 fl oz IPA beer
>
> 1 pineapple slice, as garnish
>
> 1 rosemary sprig, as garnish
>
> * Soak 1 Earl Grey teabag in half a (750 ml) bottle of Pineau des Charentes for 1½ hours.

To a cocktail shaker half-filled with medium ice cubes, add the rye, Pineau des Charentes, shrub, lemon juice, and bitters. Cover and shake. Strain into an ice-filled Collins glass and top with the beer; garnish with the pineapple and rosemary. *Makes 1*

I was introduced to Pineau des Charentes on a trip to Paris, or I should say to the 16th arrondissement—which, if you could properly describe Paris as having suburbs, is the suburbs. We were starved from the flight and anxious to get into Paris "proper." But our host had other plans: she preferred a local place. I was hesitant. This was Paris (almost), and I wanted to dine in the shadow of the Eiffel Tower. However, not only was her choice close by, but she was dating the bartender. Every step we took made me feel as if I was being lured into a trap. Once we arrived, I'll admit I was shocked—the place looked like Denny's with a bar. I decided to show off my rudimentary language skills and prove my *gastronomique* chops by ordering a glass of wine. A French wine, *mais oui.*

"*Non,*" said monsieur le bartender as he raised his eyebrows, admonishing and embracing me all in one gesture.

"Pineau," he said, sweeping the bottle from the shelf. Of course, I heard "pinot" and smugly thought my suggestion of wine was correct after all. It was not. I was served Pineau des Charentes, a lively combination of cognac and freshly pressed juice from very ripe grapes. I was entranced, and I've held onto that memory ever since. I'm pleased to see that David Delaney and other forward-thinking mixologists have taken notice of Pineau des Charentes.

BARREL-AGED BERLIONI

The Berlioni was originally created by Berlin-based bartender Gonçalo de Sousa Monteiro as a riff on that great cocktail star, the Negroni. My version was adapted from *The PDT Cocktail Book* by Jim Meehan and Chris Gall. The dark notes of barrel-aged gin in conjunction with orange bitters take this cocktail a step back toward its roots.

2 pony shots / 60 ml / 2 fl oz barrel-aged gin
½ pony shot / 15 ml / ½ fl oz Cynar or other herbaceous amaro
½ pony shot / 15 ml / ½ fl oz white vermouth
1 dash orange bitters
1 large, wide orange peel chip, as garnish

Combine the gin, Cynar, vermouth, and bitters in a mixing glass half-filled with ice. Stir until chilled and properly diluted, about 20 seconds. Julep-strain into an old-fashioned glass filled with medium ice cubes. Garnish with the orange peel, expressing its oil onto the surface, rubbing it on the rim of the glass, and then dropping it in, peel side up. *Makes 1*

Barrel-aged gin is the latest, oldest new thing out there. Once upon a time, gin was distilled at point A, then shipped in wooden barrels to point B. Naturally the qualities and quirks of the wooden vessel changed the nature of the spirit during transport, often imbuing it with a nutty palate and hues ranging from barest amber to deeply caramel.

Today barrel-aged gins are rather rare. You won't find them at just any liquor store; they tend to be very, very local. I was recently in Columbus, Ohio, where I tasted a version from Watershed Distillery. Imperial Gin offers a limited edition. Bols barrel-ages a genever that's quite good. Ransom has an Old Tom that nicely bridges the gap between genever and modern-day dry gin. Others, including Breukelen, Corsair, and Rusty Blade, occasionally have barrel-aged gins available. So look around—interest in this spirit is growing.

Barrel-aged gin works well in what I'm defining as a "savory" cocktail. It has complementing attributes of both whiskey and gin. There are the smoked vanilla and rounded texture that come from barrel-aging, balancing the sharp edges of gin's complicated beauty. And no two barrel-aged gins are quite the same.

If you can't find ready-made barrel-aged gin, get your own barrel and do the aging at home. Two-liter handcrafted oak aging barrels are available online.

DEAD GLAMOUR

Glamour never goes out of style—as proven by this cocktail from Adam Fortuna, the enthusiastic bar manager at Artusi in Seattle's Capitol Hill neighborhood. His drink has a lot going for it, from its intriguing color to the whiff of smoked spice in the nose. It's sexy and stylish. In other words, it's my kind of drink.

1 shot / 45 ml / 1½ fl oz tequila reposado
1 pony shot / 30 ml / 1 fl oz Campari
½ pony shot / 15 ml / ½ fl oz Santa Maria al Monte or other herbaceous amaro
2 dashes cardamom bitters
1 orange twist, as garnish

Combine the tequila, Campari, amaro, and bitters in a mixing glass half-filled with ice. Gently stir until chilled and properly diluted, about 20 seconds. Julep-strain into a chilled coupe or cocktail glass. Garnish with an orange twist, expressing its oil onto the surface, rubbing it onto the rim of the glass, and dropping it in, peel side up. *Makes 1*

BLACK SALT

This is another complex cocktail with dark sex appeal—smooth and bittersweet, with a full mouthfeel and a *crema* top.

2 pinches Hawaiian black lava sea salt, divided*
1 shot / 45 ml / 1½ fl oz rye
½ shot / 22½ ml / ¾ fl oz coffee liqueur
¼ pony shot / 7½ ml / ¼ fl oz Fernet-Branca
1 small egg white (optional)

* *Black lava sea salt is a blend of sea salt and purified volcanic charcoal, but another sea salt may be substituted.*

Use a mortar and pestle to grind the salt until it is roughly the texture of coarse table salt.

In a cocktail shaker, combine the bourbon, coffee liqueur, Fernet-Branca, 1 tiny pinch of black salt, and the egg white (if using). Cover and vigorously "dry shake" the ingredients about 30 seconds to combine. Uncap the shaker, fill ⅔ full with medium ice cubes, and shake vigorously again until frothy, at least 30 seconds. Using a Hawthorn strainer, double-strain the cocktail through a wire-mesh sieve into a chilled old-fashioned glass. Wait a moment for the *crema* to rise, then sprinkle another tiny pinch of black salt on top. *Makes 1*

APEROL TEQUILA SWIZZLE

This a fun drink. Maybe that's why Aperol has become the darling of the cocktail world, just in time for this Italian liqueur's centennial. It has the bitter complexity of orange peel and goes down easy. It's something they'd serve at "happy hour" in Italy, though they wouldn't call it *felice oro*. Instead, it's known as *apertivo*, and it's like an ebullient cocktail party happily scheduled every day during those possibility-filled hours between work and dinner. Like a cocktail party, the *apertivo* is certain to include *stuzzichini* (toothpick) bites, or even crunchy American-style snacks. The drinks will be light, too, designed to engage the appetite for the meal to come.

> 2 pony shots / 60 ml / 2 fl oz tequila blanco
> 1 pony shot / 30 ml / 1 fl oz Aperol
> 2 or 3 dashes grapefruit or orange bitters
> ¼ to ⅜ cup / 2 to 3 fl oz club soda
> 1 pinch coarse salt
> 1 grapefruit twist, as garnish

Fill a wine goblet or highball glass with medium ice cubes; add the tequila, Aperol, and bitters. Use a swizzle stick or straw to stir the ingredients until just blended. Top with club soda and a pinch of salt; stir gently and garnish with a grapefruit twist. Serve with the swizzle stick or straw. *Makes 1*

OFF-WHITE NEGRONI

From Italian *apertivo* to French *aperitif*, this Off-White Negroni features a bitter liqueur that is an emerging star in the bitter-spirits category. In France, it is served over ice before dinner, and it was immortalized in the Picasso collage *Glass and a Bottle of Suze*. Don't let the pale hue fool you. This bitter liqueur gets its bite from the rootstock of the gentian plant. It's used here by Nathan Hazard in a riff on a classic.

> 1 shot / 45 ml / 1½ fl oz Ransom or other Old Tom gin
> ½ shot / 22½ ml / ¾ fl oz gentian liqueur such as Suze
> ½ shot / 22½ ml / ¾ fl oz Cocchi Americano
> 1 lemon peel chip, as garnish

Combine the gin, gentian liqueur, and Cocchi in a mixing glass half-filled with ice. Gently stir until chilled and properly diluted, about 20 seconds. Julep-strain into a chilled coupe. Garnish with a lemon chip, expressing its oil onto the surface, rubbing it on the glass rim, and dropping it in the drink, peel side up. *Makes 1*

HANKY PANKY

Here's my version of this classic cocktail from London's famed *Savoy Cocktail Book*. As was *en vogue* during Prohibition, this drink has a rather scandalous name. One can easily imagine the "wets" of the Savoy Hotel's American Bar laughing while hoisting a glass to America's dry "era of temperance." This cocktail's name was particularly suggestive because it was likely to have been poured by a female bartender by the name of Ada Coleman—"Coley" to the drinking set at the bar. Not only was she that rare female in a male-dominated profession, but she was credited by Ted Haigh in his excellent book *Vintage Spirits and Forgotten Cocktails* with making the American Bar a destination.

> 1 shot / 45 ml / 1½ fl oz dry gin
> 1 shot / 45 ml / 1½ fl oz red vermouth
> ¼ pony shot / 15 ml / ¼ fl oz Fernet-Branca
> 1 orange twist, as garnish

Combine the gin, vermouth, and Fernet-Branca in a mixing glass half-filled with ice. Stir until chilled and properly diluted, about 20 seconds. Strain into a chilled coupe or cocktail glass. Garnish with an orange twist, expressing its oil expressed onto the surface, rubbing it on the glass rim, and dropping it in, peel side up. *Makes 1*

Like so many cocktail books from the "golden age," the *Savoy Cocktail Book* (1930) reads more like a list than a biography. Oh, but what an important list it is. Its author, Harry Craddock, was then and remains now a tastemaker (though he was little more than a bar-back when Ada was impresario). Many cocktails lived on (or died off) based on this book, helping define the craft cocktail movement of today.

Ted Haigh's *Vintage Spirits and Forgotten Cocktails* (2004, 2009) is a well-edited mini-encyclopedia of sorts, the perfect snapshot of a bygone era for modern readers. In just 100 recipes, it's arguably singularly responsible for bringing the vogue back to the cocktail world.

SMOKY

Smoky cocktails aren't for the faint of palate, but smoldering mezcals and peaty scotches are gaining a new audience as people's acceptance of complex flavors grows. Bartenders have noticed this trend and are incorporating sooty sensations into their bar lists in all sorts of ways, both new and traditional.

THE LONG GOODBYE

The Long Goodbye is a cocktail from Jay Porter that has an appropriately long, smoky finish. It appears on the menu of his San Diego restaurant El Take It Easy. The long finish comes from mezcal, a 100 percent agave spirit that's gathering quite a bit of notice among the culinary set. Mezcal can be gorgeously complex and endlessly intriguing. Still, many folks are bewildered by this spirit, despite its having been dubbed "The Next Big Thing in Booze" by many writers in the spirits world. Part of the confusion stems from the fact that not all mezcal is tequila—though all tequila can be classified as mezcal. Tequila is a form of mezcal that by law can be produced only in designated areas of western Mexico.

So what, then, is mezcal? Despite its newfound fame, mezcal in the broadest sense is the precursor to tequila, much as rye is to bourbon. These days, tequila is mostly produced in large factories, and its flavor profile has been homogenized. This isn't necessarily a bad thing—there's something to be said for a well-made, smoothly elegant tequila—but mezcal is still mostly made by hand, by a far more humble process of distilling the agave plant. A young mezcal, known as a *jovan*, gains its smoky backbone when the agave is roasted in *palenques*, or rock-lined pits, prior to distilling. Though not typical, some mezcals are aged and become known as *reposado*. But Jay prefers to use a young blanco variety to show the raw essence of mezcal.

> 2 pony shots / 60 ml / 2 fl oz mezcal blanco
> 2 tbsp / 1 fl oz freshly squeezed lime juice
> 1 tbsp / ½ fl oz herbal lemon syrup, using mint (see page 7)

Combine the mezcal, lime juice, and lemon syrup in a cocktail shaker ⅔ filled with ice. Shake vigorously and strain into a chilled coupe glass. *Makes 1*

AUTUMN ASH

The Autumn Ash is a modern-day scotch cocktail. Back in the days of Madison Avenue's *Mad Men*–style boardrooms, scotch meant blended whiskey—that's whiskey with an "e." In fact, whiskey was blended to intentionally give it an air of conformity. Some brands were naturally better than others, but all were pretty much after the same prize: the loyalty of the (mostly) men who swigged the stuff as a matter of status. Over the decades, the status of blended whiskey has suffered at the peat-stained hands of very good single malt whisky—that's whisky without the "e." But the tables are turning once again. Blended whisky (with or without an "e") is turning up on top shelves everywhere. It's a terrific choice for complex, smoke-tinged savory cocktails. I love the restrained way the "smoke" in this cocktail wafts into your consciousness a millisecond after the fact.

2 pony shots / 60 ml / 2 fl oz blended scotch whisky
1 pony shot / 30 ml / 1 fl oz apple brandy
¼ pony shot / 7½ ml / ¼ fl oz elderflower liqueur
2 dashes orange bitters
1 lemon twist, as garnish

Combine the scotch, apple brandy, elderflower liqueur, and bitters in a mixing glass half-filled with ice. Stir until chilled and properly diluted, about 20 seconds. Julep-strain into a chilled coupe or cocktail glass. Garnish with a lemon twist, expressing its oil onto the surface, rubbing it on the glass rim, and dropping it in, peel side up. *Makes 1*

BETTER WITH BACON

… and I mean everything.

2 slices crispy bacon, divided
1 shot / 45 ml / 1½ fl oz rye
2 tbsp / 1 fl oz lime juice
1 tbsp/ ½ fl oz simple syrup
3 drops liquid smoke (use an eye dropper, not the shaker top on the bottle)

Crumble a piece of bacon and place it in a pint glass of a Boston shaker. Add the rye, lime juice, simple syrup, and liquid smoke. Allow the mixture to sit for about 10 minutes then strain through a paper towel into a cocktail shaker ⅔ filled with ice. Discard the solids. Cover and shake vigorously. Using a Hawthorn strainer, double-strain the cocktail through a wire-mesh sieve into a chilled cocktail glass. Lay the remaining bacon slice across the top of the glass to nibble on. *Makes 1*

SMOG CUTTER

This is a Dan Greenbaum recipe from his bar, The Beagle, which is definitely located in New York despite all the Internet indications that it's in Portland, Oregon. Maybe the myth came about because Dan's partner in the place, Matt Piacentini, is a Portlander. Regardless, it may account for the fact that I often see this terrific bar referred to as The Beagle NYC.

1 (⅛-inch) slice English cucumber
1 tbsp / ½ fl oz freshly squeezed lime juice
1 tbsp / ½ fl oz TomR's tonic syrup or other quinine syrup (available online)
1 tbsp / ½ fl oz ginger syrup (see page 7)
½ shot / 22 ml / ¾ fl oz mezcal blanco
Negra Modelo beer, as needed

In a sturdy, thick-bottomed pint glass from a Boston shaker, use a bar muddler to crush the cucumber, lime juice, tonic syrup, and ginger syrup into a fragrant, pulpy mush. Pour in the mezcal.

Fill the metal part of the Boston shaker ⅔ full with ice. Pour the muddled mezcal mixture (including pulp) over the ice and then cap the shaker with the pint glass. Shake vigorously until well chilled. Using a Hawthorn strainer, double-strain the cocktail through a wire-mesh sieve into an ice-filled Collins glass. Fill the glass with beer and stir gently to combine. Serve with a straw.   *Makes 1*

SMOKEJUMPER

This is a cocktail from Jacob Grier (see page 59). It's made smoky with lapsang souchong tea, a black tea dried over burning pinewood.

2 pony shots / 60 ml / 2 fl oz dry gin
1½ tbsp / ¾ oz freshly squeezed lemon juice
1 tbsp / ½ oz yellow Chartreuse
1 tbsp / ½ oz lapsang souchong syrup*
1 lemon twist, as garnish

* To make the syrup, mix 1 cup freshly brewed lapsang souchong tea with 1 cup sugar until the sugar has dissolved. Makes about 1¼ cups. Store the extra syrup covered and refrigerated up to 1 month.

Combine the gin, lemon juice, Chartreuse, and syrup in a cocktail shaker ⅔ filled with ice. Shake vigorously. Strain into an old-fashioned glass filled with ice cubes. Garnish with the lemon twist.   *Makes 1*

THE CHAPARRAL

This is my own invention, if there is such a thing. Cocktails, even the best of them, often rely on those that came before.

Peel from 1 red or pink grapefruit, roughly chopped
Water, as needed
¾ cup sugar, divided
1 tbsp lightly crushed salt, preferably Hawaiian alaea pink salt
¼ peeled red or pink grapefruit, cut into 4 chunks
6 large sage leaves, divided
2 pony shots / 60 ml / 2 fl oz tequila blanco
1 scant barspoon spiced syrup, using black pepper (see page 7)
½ pony shot / 15 ml / ½ fl oz mezcal reposado
1 sage sprig, as garnish

Place the oven rack in the center position and preheat the oven to 225°F. Line a baking sheet with parchment paper.

Place the grapefruit peel in a small saucepan, pour in enough water to cover, and add ¼ cup sugar; bring to a boil. Drain off the syrup and repeat the process two more times, using all the sugar. Strain out the peels and spread them in a single layer on the lined baking sheet. Place in the preheated oven to dry completely, 2 hours or longer. Watch carefully—you want the peels to remain pink but be totally dry and crisp enough to snap. Once the peels are dried, grind them into a powder.

Mix 1 tablespoon dried grapefruit powder and the pink salt on a saucer. Moisten the rim of a double old-fashioned glass and press it into the mixture until the mixture adheres. Fill the glass with medium ice cubes; set aside.

Place the grapefruit chunks and sage leaves in a sturdy, thick-bottomed pint glass from a Boston shaker. Use a bar muddler to crush them until most of the juice is extracted—it's okay if the grapefruit pulp is still partly intact. Pour in the tequila and spoon in the black pepper syrup. Stir lightly to combine and to remove all the syrup from the spoon.

Fill the metal part of the Boston shaker ⅔ full with ice. Pour the muddled tequila mixture (including pulp) over the ice cubes and cap the shaker with the pint glass. Shake vigorously until well chilled. Using a Hawthorn strainer, double-strain the cocktail through a wire-mesh sieve into an ice-filled old-fashioned glass. Pour the mezcal onto the drink over the back of a barspoon. Garnish with sage sprig. *Makes 1*

THE HICKORY STICK

This drink comes from Travis Owens, the talented owner/mixologist for Curio at Harvest Pizzeria in Columbus, Ohio. This drink shows real finesse in the handling of its diverse elements. The woodsy rye-driven bourbon is layered with Fernet-Branca, two kinds of vermouth, and Campari-like Luxardo Bitter—basically booze on top of booze that somehow comes together to make a well-balanced, subtly smoky cocktail.

1 shot / 45 ml / 1½ fl oz bourbon
¼ pony shot / 7½ ml / ¼ fl oz Fernet-Branca
¼ pony shot / 7½ ml / ¼ fl oz Luxardo Bitter (or substitute Campari)
½ pony shot / 15 ml / ½ fl oz red vermouth
¼ pony shot / 7½ ml / ¼ fl oz white vermouth
¼ pony shot / 7½ ml / ¼ fl oz simple syrup (see page 6)
4–7 drops liquid smoke (use an eye dropper, not the shaker top on the bottle)
1 large, wide lemon peel chip, as garnish

Place 2 medium ice cubes in an old-fashioned glass. Set aside.

Combine the bourbon, Fernet-Branca, Luxardo Bitter, both vermouths, and the simple syrup in a cocktail shaker with ⅔ filled ice and shake vigorously until well chilled. Strain into the prepared glass. Garnish with the lemon chip, expressing its oil onto the surface, rubbing it onto the rim of the glass, and dropping it in, peel side up. *Makes 1*

OLD HICKORY

Here's a very old drink made only with fortified wine and bitters. It is not a particularly smoky cocktail in the expected sense. But it does sit heavy on the tongue and linger. This version was adapted from Maison Premiere in Brooklyn, New York.

1 shot / 45 ml / 1½ fl oz red vermouth
1 pony shot / 30 ml / 1 fl oz white vermouth
2 dashes Peychaud's bitters or Aromatic "House" Bitters (see page10)
2 dashes orange bitters
1 orange twist, as garnish

Fill an old-fashioned glass with ice. Build the drink by adding both vermouths and both bitters one at a time, swirling to combine. Garnish with the orange twist, expressing its oil onto the surface, rubbing it onto the rim of the glass, and dropping it in the drink, peel side up. *Makes 1*

RICKEY OAXAQUEÑA

Rickey Oaxaqueña sounds like an interesting fellow. But this Rickey isn't a Cuban bandleader; in fact, he's not even a person. Rickey is a refreshing style of cocktail similar to a Collins or a fizz, with an obvious difference. Rickey (the drink) doesn't traditionally include any sweeteners, instead making a powerfully sour statement. This version from Nathan Hazard stays true to that tradition and is made particularly savory with the addition of a coffee and cigarettes–inspired infused mezcal.

2 pony shots / 60 ml / 2 fl oz coffee-infused mezcal blanco (see page 12)
2 tbsp / 1 fl oz freshly squeezed lime juice
1 or 2 dashes Bittermens Xocolatl Mole Bitters (available online, optional)
¼ to ⅛ cup / 2 to 3 fl oz club soda
1 lime wedge

Fill a highball glass with medium ice cubes. Build the drink by adding the mezcal, lime juice, and bitters (if using) one at a time to the glass. Top with club soda and stir gently. Squeeze the lime wedge over the drink, then drop it in. *Makes 1*

THE CHRISTOPHER OAXACAN

Yeah, I know you're laughing, but this is another serious drink from Travis Owens (see page 103).

1 shot / 45 ml / 1½ fl oz mezcal blanco
½ shot / 22½ ml / ¾ fl oz red vermouth
¼ pony shot / 7½ ml / ¼ fl oz Cocchi Americano
¼ pony shot / 7½ ml / ¼ fl oz Campari
1 or 2 dashes orange bitters

Combine the mezcal, vermouth, Cocchi, Campari, and bitters in a cocktail shaker ⅔ full of ice. Shake vigorously until well chilled. Strain into a chilled coupe or cocktail glass. *Makes 1*

PENICILLIN COCKTAIL

New York bartender Sam Ross's instant classic Penicillin Cocktail is much more comforting than its medicinal-sounding name. It embellishes the traditional healing flavors of whisky, honey, and lemon with ginger and a whiff of something smoky. The smoky aroma comes from Islay scotch whisky—renowned for its peaty, briny, and sometimes medicinal flavors, a sure antidote to chilly nights. Like the original version, mine is served on the rocks, but it can take on further curative properties when stirred into a shot of very hot, very strong tea. In which case, skip the step of shaking the ingredients with ice.

1 small chunk fresh ginger
2 pony shots / 60 ml / 2 fl oz blended scotch whisky
1 pony shot / 30 ml / 1 fl oz freshly squeezed lemon juice
¼ pony shot / 7½ ml / ¼ fl oz ginger and black pepper agave syrup (see page 7)
Drizzle of Lagavulin or other Islay single malt scotch whisky

Rub the ginger along the rim of an old-fashioned glass, then drop it in. Place 2 or 3 medium ice cubes in the glass; set aside.

In a cocktail shaker ⅔ filled with medium ice cubes, combine the blended scotch, lemon juice, and agave syrup. Shake vigorously, then strain into the prepared glass. Pour in the Islay scotch over the back of a barspoon so that it floats atop the drink, creating that distinctive aroma.   *Makes 1*

Islay (*EYE-luh*) refers to an island off the coast of Scotland that produces distinctively smoky scotch whisky. The west coast of the island is one of the most appreciated areas in the world among single malt lovers. It's here that local barley, yeast, and water are brought together to begin the process of germination, turning starch into sugar. The resulting mixture is referred to as malt. The malt is then dried with smoke and heat from peat—a mossy accumulation of partially decayed vegetation that builds up in the bogs of Islay. The burning peat halts the germination process, and the malt develops a smoky, peaty, often briny flavor. The result is made into mash, then distilled and aged by world-renowned producers such as Laphroaig, Lagavulin, and Ardberg.

RICH

Rich cocktails are a decadent way to imbibe. I find them delightful at the end of a delicious evening. However, rich and decadent need not mean sweet and cloying—luxury can be mixed into the glass in many different ways. Modern bartenders have brought new levels of sophistication to this category of drink, though the concept has been around for a long time. Eggs and cream were once added to drinks to mask the quirks of the cheap booze served at some speakeasies. Flips and nogs come to mind, as does the brandy Alexander.

CAMPARI ALEXANDER

I saw this on the menu at Bobby Heugel, Kevin Floyd, and Steve Flippo's excellent Houston bar, Anvil, way back in 2009. Its memory has lingered. This is a smart combination, very much like deeply dark bittersweet chocolate. Similar to the brandy Alexander, it has just three ingredients, so it's easy to reproduce at home. Unlike the traditional version that features its ingredients in equal proportions, my taste-testing told me that a 2:1:1 ratio brings out the bitter better. I've also finished my version with a light dusting of unsweetened cocoa powder, which helps this drink taste just like dirt. Really good dirt.

2 pony shots / 60 ml / 2 fl oz Campari
2 tbsp / 1 fl oz dark crème de cacao
2 tbsp / 1 fl oz heavy cream
Unsweetened cocoa powder, to taste, as garnish (optional)

Add the Campari, crème de cacao, and cream to a cocktail shaker ⅔ filled with ice. Shake vigorously until frothy. Using a Hawthorn strainer, double-strain the cocktail through a wire-mesh sieve into a double old-fashioned glass. Allow the foam to rise, then garnish with a sprinkling of unsweetened cocoa powder (if using). *Makes 1*

THE ALEXANDER

This rich gin drink is an earlier version of its brandied brother. First published in Hugo Ensslin's *Recipes for Mixed Drinks* (1917), it's not as complex as Bobby Heugel's creation (above), but the botanicals in gin add an unexpectedly savory note to this creamy concoction.

1 pony shot / 30 ml / 1 fl oz dry gin
2 tbsp / 1 fl oz white crème de cacao
2 tbsp / 1 fl oz heavy cream

Pour all the ingredients into a cocktail shaker ⅔ full of ice. Shake vigorously until frothy. Using a Hawthorn strainer, double-strain the cocktail through a wire-mesh sieve into a chilled coupe or cocktail glass. *Makes 1*

COOL REVIVAL

The Cool Revival is a cool cocktail. It's just one example of the creative juice that bar manager Jaymee Mandeville channels into her inspired seasonal cocktail lists at Drago Centro in downtown Los Angeles. What I like about this cocktail, and why I chose to include it in this book, is how deliciously it illustrates how the demand for all things fresh, seasonal, and local has carried over from the kitchen to the bar. It has created a new trend in cocktails that goes beyond savory and can best be described as culinary cocktails—challenging the palate without a whiff of pomposity.

4 (⅛-inch) slices unpeeled English cucumber

2 pony shots / 60 ml / 2 fl oz rye

½ pony shot / 15 ml / ½ fl oz Cynar or other herbaceous amaro

1 tbsp / ½ fl oz yuzu juice, freshly squeezed or bottled*

1 tbsp / ½ fl oz herbal lemon syrup, using dill (see page 7)

Dill and Lemon Meringue (recipe below)

1 pinch grated lemon zest, as garnish

1 sprig fresh dill sprig, as garnish

Lime juice can be substituted for yuzu juice. For information about yuzu, see the Golden Ale recipe on page 28.

In a sturdy, thick-bottomed pint glass from a Boston shaker, use a bar muddler to crush the cucumber slices until most of the juice has been extracted and you have a fragrant, pulpy mush. Add the rye, Cynar, yuzu juice, and herbal lemon syrup, swirling to combine.

Fill the metal part of the Boston shaker ⅔ full of ice. Pour the muddled rye mixture (including pulp) over the ice cubes, then cap the shaker with the pint glass. Shake vigorously until well chilled.

Using a Hawthorn strainer, double-strain the cocktail through a wire-mesh sieve into an ice-filled mini-Mason jar or old-fashioned glass. Heap some of the dill and lemon meringue on top. Garnish with the lemon zest and dill sprig. *Makes 1*

DILL AND LEMON MERINGUE

¼ cup / 2 fl oz herbal lemon syrup, using dill (see page 7)

1 egg white

In a small bowl, mix the dill and lemon simple syrup with the egg white. Use either an electric mixer or whipped-cream dispenser to bring the mixture to a soft-peaked meringue consistency. Let rest for at least 6 minutes.

THE GUAYABERA

Long before Sandals was a chain of resorts, *huaraches* were shoes worn in hot climates, and the *guayabera* was a loose fitting four-pocketed gentleman's work shirt with a bit of ventilation designed into it. These days you're more likely to be wearing those sandals with linen pants while quaffing H. Joseph Ehrmann's liquid version of The Guayabera. It's every bit as tropical as the shirt and twice as cool.

The cocktail's creator, the mixologist behind San Francisco's Elixir cocktail bar, says the drink "sounds like guacamole and tastes like a lounge chair by the pool." It has a rich, smooth mouthfeel from the avocado, sharpened by ginger and cilantro. There's more than enough acidity to let this surprising cocktail sit nicely alongside that cold shellfish or ceviche I know you've planned for lunch.

4 heaping barspoons ripe avocado
Half a (½-inch) slice peeled fresh pineapple, chopped
    (or 2 tbsp / 1 fl oz pineapple juice)
3-finger pinch cilantro leaves
3 dime-size pieces peeled fresh ginger
1 shot / 45 ml / 1½ fl oz cucumber-infused vodka
    (see Mild-Flavored Vegetable Infusion, page 12)
2 tbsp / 1 fl oz freshly squeezed lemon juice
2 tbsp / 1 fl oz agave syrup*
1 (10½-oz) glassful of cracked ice (for frozen version only)
1 lime wedge, as garnish
1 cilantro sprig, as garnish

Mix agave nectar and water in a 1:1 ratio.

On the rocks: In a sturdy, thick-bottomed pint glass from a Boston shaker, use a bar muddler to crush the avocado, pineapple, cilantro leaves, and ginger into a fragrant, pulpy mush. Pour in the vodka, lemon juice, and agave syrup, swirling to combine.

Fill the metal part of the Boston shaker ⅔ full with ice. Pour the muddled vodka mixture (including pulp) over the ice; cap with the pint glass. Shake vigorously until well chilled. Using a Hawthorn strainer, double-strain the cocktail through a wire-mesh sieve into an ice-filled double old-fashioned or highball glass. Garnish with the lime and cilantro.

Frozen: Place everything except the lime wedge and cilantro sprig in a blender (preferably a Vitamix Barboss). Blend thoroughly (on the #3 setting, if using the Barboss). Pour into a chilled glass. Garnish with the lime and cilantro. *Makes 1*

AMARO FLIP

Today a Flip refers to a drink that is shaken with a whole egg, or sometimes cream. These drinks are usually served cold nowadays, but originally Flips were warm—heated by a red-hot iron plunged into the drink, making it bubble and become frothy.

My version is made with amaro, a class of bitter Italian digestifs. When "flipped" with a whole egg, an amaro can take on a bitter richness similar to unsweetened cocoa. It's best served after a luxurious meal.

2 shots / 90 ml / 3 fl oz Italian amaro liqueur such as Fernet-Branca or Averna
2 dashes Miracle Mile Chocolate Chili Bitters (available online, optional)
1 small egg
Freshly grated nutmeg, as garnish

Combine the amaro, bitters (if using), and egg in a cocktail shaker. Cover and "dry shake" for about 30 seconds to combine. Uncap the shaker and fill ⅔ full with ice; shake vigorously until well chilled and frothy, at least 30 seconds. Using a Hawthorn strainer, double-strain the cocktail through a wire-mesh sieve into a wine goblet. Wait a moment for the foam to rise, then garnish with grated nutmeg. *Makes 1*

Let's face it. We're all human, and we occasionally overindulge—particularly when we sit down to a large, special-occasion meal. In trying to stretch out that special moment, we sometimes simply eat too much. Way too much.

Enter the digestif. Digestifs are typically served after a meal, and they are different from the sweet little nips often paired with dessert. They're not like grappa or cognac, either, designed to continue the alcoholic buzz of overindulgence well into the night.

Digestifs are intended to soothe the overindulged belly by assisting in digestion or quelling a queasy stomach. The very best of them, in my opinion, are the Italian *digestivos*, collectively known as *amari* and enjoyed singly as *amaro*. The Italians take their digestive health seriously. There are hundreds of amari produced in Italy. Derived from quinine, they are typically bitter. They generally include herbs, roots, flowers, and spices in some proprietary formulation, giving them complex flavor profiles. It's this complexity that makes them wonderful cocktail ingredients, from Averna, with a bite that's wrapped in a veil of something sweet, through bracingly bitter Fernet-Branca.

CHARTREUSE AND THE CHOCOLATE FACTORY

This is not a shy drink. Its rich, strong flavors are layered with bitter chocolate notes, the herbaceous tones of Chartreuse, and a distinctive peat-smudged smokiness. Chocolate may not be the first flavor you think of when you hear "savory," but chocolate wasn't always candy. Ancient Aztecs ground cacao beans with spices to make *xocoatl*, a drink that was a little spicy and not at all sweet. I can't help but be reminded of it when I taste this darkly rich, slightly bitter modern cocktail from David Wolowidnyk, bar manager at West Restaurant + Bar in Vancouver, Canada.

David starts the preparation with a cacao nib–infused bourbon. Cacao is naturally bitter, and when it's infused into the sweet spice of bourbon you've really got something going on—sippable all by itself. The process is easy, or I can recommend Benjamin Prichard's Double Chocolate Bourbon Whiskey, from a small-batch producer in Tennessee.

¼ pony shot / 7½ ml / ¼ fl oz scotch whisky, as rinse
1 shot / 45 ml / 1½ fl oz bourbon infused with cacao nibs (recipe below)
½ pony shot / 15 ml / ½ fl oz green Chartreuse
½ pony shot / 15 ml / ½ fl oz Cynar or other herbaceous amaro
1 dash walnut bitters

Pour the scotch into an old-fashioned glass and "turn" the glass, rolling the liquid until the inside is well coated; pour out the excess. This is known as "rinsing" the glass. Place a single large or several medium ice cubes in the glass. Set aside.

Combine the infused bourbon, Chartreuse, Cynar, and walnut bitters in a mixing glass half-filled with ice. Gently stir until chilled and properly diluted, about 20 seconds. Julep-strain into the prepared glass. *Makes 1*

CACAO BOURBON

Cacao nibs are pieces of the beans that have been roasted and hulled. They're used in making chocolate and may be purchased in specialty markets and online. Look for the plain ingredient, as opposed to chocolate-covered snack-style nibs.

1 (750 ml) bottle bourbon
½ cup cacao nibs

Combine the bourbon and cacao nibs in a large jar. Cover and let infuse for 3 days. Working in batches, strain the infused liquor through a coffee filter to remove any particles.

STRONG

Strong cocktails are much more than just good, stiff belts. They have a glamorous allure but must be impeccably made to keep from becoming brutes. They're for those of us who like to sip our drinks slowly and enjoy their assertive alcohol-forward power.

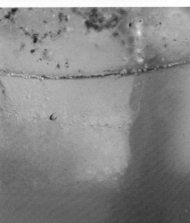

CLASSIC MARTINI

A true Classic Martini is made with gin (sorry, it just is). The aromatic botanicals of juniper, citrus peel, and cardamom make gin a natural in savory mixology. The same sorts of flavorful components found their way into herb and spice—infused vermouth. Without too much effort, the two come together to give us the sublime martini.

2 pony shots / 60 ml / 2 fl oz dry gin
½ pony shot / 15 ml / ½ fl oz white vermouth
2 or 3 drops orange bitters
1 cocktail olive or 1 lemon twist, as garnish

Add gin and vermouth to a mixing glass half-filled with ice. Gently stir until well chilled and properly diluted, about 20 seconds. Julep-strain into a chilled cocktail glass and garnish with an olive or lemon twist. *Makes 1*

DRY MARTINI

2 pony shots / 60 ml / 2 fl oz dry gin
½ pony shot / 15 ml / ½ fl oz white vermouth
1 cocktail olive or 1 lemon twist, as garnish

EXTRA-DRY MARTINI

2 pony shots / 60 ml / 2 fl oz dry gin
¼ pony shot / 7½ ml / ¼ fl oz white vermouth
1 cocktail olive or 1 lemon twist, as garnish

"PERFECT" MARTINI (This is its name, not a declaration from me.)

2 pony shots / 60 ml / 2 fl oz dry gin
½ pony shot / 15 ml / ½ fl oz white vermouth
½ pony shot / 15 ml / ½ fl oz red vermouth
1 orange slice, as garnish

SMOKY MARTINI

2 pony shots / 60 ml / 2 fl oz dry gin
¼ pony shot / 7½ ml / ¼ fl oz single malt scotch
1 barspoon white vermouth
1 lemon twist, as garnish

GIBSON

The Gibson is not exactly a martini. The obvious difference is the garnish—a pickled pearl onion. But to me, the real distinction is that a Gibson should be served a lot drier than a proper martini. That's why this cocktail prefers to be finished with an onion rather than an olive. There are stories of just how this cocktail *supposedly* got its name. Some offer it up as a complicated ruse designed to keep a teetotaler from mixing up his onion garnished water-filled coupe glass with all the olive-soaked martinis on the bar. But I've also heard a version that had American artist Charles Dana Gibson decorating his martini with two delicate white onion orbs as a representation of the female form.

2½ pony shots / 75 ml / 2½ fl oz dry gin
½ pony shot / 15 ml / ½ fl oz white vermouth
2 or 3 pickled pearl onions, as garnish

Combine the gin and vermouth in a mixing glass half-filled with ice. Gently stir until chilled and properly diluted, about 20 seconds. Julep-strain into a chilled cocktail glass and drop in the onions. *Makes 1*

VESPER

The Vesper actually comes from James Bond, a man of many talents, and the world has come to embrace this liqurious libation. Though I have to admit that the Vesper has never done much for me. I suspect this is because a key ingredient Kina Lillet is no longer made. In 1986, Lillet reformulated it to a less alcoholic and less bitter version now known as Lillet Blanc. Without the pronounced bitterness from Kina Lillet, the Vesper as a cocktail seems a bit brutish for my tastes. However, I've lately tried it with another appertif that is enjoying a resurgence itself right now. Cocchi Aperitivo Americano is said to be the most similar product in existence to the old-formula of Kina Lillet, which makes the Vesper intriguing to me once again.

2 shots / 90 ml / 3 fl oz dry gin
1 pony shot / 30 ml / 1 fl oz vodka
½ pony shot / 15 ml / ½ fl oz Cocchi Americano
3 drops Bittermens Hopped Grapefruit Bitters (available online, optional)
1 long, thin spiral of lemon peel, as garnish

Add the gin, vodka, Cocchi, and bitters (if using) to a cocktail shaker ⅔ filled with ice. Shake vigorously. Strain into a chilled cocktail glass and garnish with the lemon peel. *Makes 1*

HAIR (RAISING) TONIC

The Hair (Raising) Tonic may have some medicinal value (or it may not). You see, bitters were once elixirs designed to cure whatever ailed you. Later they were marketed as tonics, and some were said to promote the growth of hair—hence the name of my cocktail cure-all. I can't promise it will grow hair, but I can't promise it won't, either.

2½ pony shots / 75 ml / 2½ fl oz Ransom or other Old Tom gin
½ pony shot / 15 ml / 1 fl oz aquavit, preferably Linie
¼ pony shot / 7½ ml / ¼ fl oz spiced syrup, using dark espresso beans (see page 7)
1 dash Angostura bitters, or Aromatic "House" Bitters (see page 10)
1 dash orange bitters
Finely grated nutmeg, as garnish

Combine the gin, aquavit, coffee syrup, and both bitters in a mixing glass half-filled with ice. Stir until chilled and properly diluted, about 20 seconds. Julep-strain into an old-fashioned glass filled with medium ice cubes. Garnish with a generous grating of nutmeg. *Makes 1*

Aquavit *(AH-kwuh-veet)* is a Scandinavian liquor with the assertiveness of caraway. There are several aquavit cocktails in this book, because the spirit lends itself well to savory applications.

Norwegians make an especially interesting version that I thought deserved a bit of discussion. Linie *(LINN-yuh)* is a style of aquavit whose journey is unlike any spirit I know. Aquavit starts as a clear potato-based liquor similar to vodka. Botanicals such as caraway, dill, and cumin are added, and the spirit known as aquavit (aqua vitae in Latin, meaning "water of life") is born. To become Linie, the aquavit is placed in oak sherry casks and loaded onto ships for a trip "down under." But Australia isn't the final destination. Once it has arrived, it quietly waits to be shipped right back to Norway, because the purpose of the journey is to send the liquid over the equator. It's said to acquire a particularly rich flavor as it sloshes around the barrel to the unique rhythm only an ocean journey can provide. Really.

NEON ROSE

Miracle Mile Bitters is a small-batch, handcrafted elixir produced in Los Angeles by Louis Anderman. He's been making this cocktail and then barrel-aging it in the same barrels he used for the new bitters. While you don't need to barrel-age the cocktail to enjoy it, can you imagine how good it would be if you did?

2 pony shots / 60 ml / 2 fl oz dry gin

1 pony shot / 30 ml / 1 oz Cocchi Americano

2 dashes Miracle Mile Forbidden Bitters (available online), or Angostura or
    Aromatic "House" Bitters (see page 10)

1 large, wide orange chip, as garnish (flamed, if you want to get fancy)

Combine the gin, Cocchi, and bitters in a mixing glass half-filled with ice. Gently stir until chilled and properly diluted, about 20 seconds. Julep-strain into a chilled coupe or cocktail glass. Garnish with the orange chip, expressed or flamed (see directions below) and then dropped into the drink. *Makes 1*

How to "Flame" Citrus Peel

1. Cut a chip of citrus peel about the size of a quarter and a bit thicker than if you were creating a twist.

2. Light a wooden match and hold it a few inches above your cocktail.

3. Hold the peel, colored side down, just above the flame. Heat the oils in the peel by hovering it over the flame.

4. Express the oils into the cocktail through the flame by squeezing and twisting the peel between your thumb and forefinger in a single motion. The oils will ignite in a quick, bright light show as they scent the top of the cocktail. Enjoy the applause.

SCOFFLAW

That's a fun word. But it wasn't supposed to be. In late 1923, during the Prohibition era, the *Boston Herald* held a contest offering $200 to whoever developed the best word to "stab awake the conscience" and publicly describe "a lawless drinker of illegally made or illegally obtained liquor." The requirements? The new word needed to be just one or two syllables and thoroughly brand the drinker as a no-goodnik, someone who shamelessly scoffs at the law. More than 25,000 entries were received.

The winner? Scofflaw, of course, a simple combination of two existing words. Three days after the announcement of the winning entry, ex-pat Americans at Harry's Bar in Paris did a little rebranding of the word, and this cocktail was born. As noted by Boozehound author Jason Wilson, the original recipe calls for grenadine instead of green Chartreuse. The savory edge of Chartreuse was his idea, and I have adopted it.

1 shot / 45 ml / 1½ fl oz rye
1 pony shot / 30 ml / 1 fl oz white vermouth
½ shot / 22½ ml / ¾ fl oz green Chartreuse
1½ tbsp / ¾ fl oz freshly squeezed lemon juice
2 or 3 dashes orange bitters
1 large, wide orange peel chip, as garnish

To a cocktail shaker ⅔ filled with ice, add the rye, vermouth, Chartreuse, lemon juice, and bitters. Shake vigorously until well chilled, then strain into a chilled coupe or cocktail glass. Garnish with the orange chip, expressing its oil onto the surface, rubbing it onto the rim of the glass, and dropping it in the drink, peel side up. *Makes 1*

DORFLINGER

Forget Harvey Wallbanger—I'll have a Dorflinger, another oldie but goodie. It comes from *The Old Waldorf-Astoria Bar Book* (1935). All I can say is, brace yourself, it's gonna hurt.

2 pony shots / 60 ml / 2 fl oz dry gin
1 pony shot / 30 ml / 1 fl oz absinthe
1 dash orange bitters

Add the gin, absinthe, and bitters to a mixing glass half-filled with ice. Gently stir until the cocktail is well chilled and properly diluted, about 20 seconds. Julep-strain into a chilled cocktail glass. *Makes 1*

THE FATAL HOUR

I give you The Fatal Hour, a drink its creator calls a "fermentation cocktail." When I started this project, one of the first people I contacted was Dave Whitton from Villains Tavern in Los Angeles. Though it's in a slightly *unsavory* section of town, this popular bar was the first place I thought of when I considered the word "savory." Dave's creations embrace savory elements in combinations that stretch the genre.

I started by asking just what savory meant to him. "Well-aged high-proof bourbon," he said. He went on to explain that savory cocktails had to be layered between aroma, body, and finish. He expects these elements to play with your palate but not stick around. In his words, a savory cocktail should "trick you into thinking it's harmless (soft and subtle), only to find that the heat in the body is eye lifting—easing it into a long, long finish . . ."

> 2 pony shots / 60 ml / 2 fl oz rye
> ¾ pony shot / 22½ ml / ¾ fl oz Amaro Nonino or other herbaceous amaro
> 2 dashes of Miracle Mile Chocolate Chile Bitters (available online)
> 1 cocktail cherry, preferably Luxardo, as "food" for the rye

Combine the rye, amaro, and bitters in mixing glass half-filled with ice. Let chill about 20 seconds, then julep-strain into a chilled coupe. Use a barspoon to scoop up a cherry with some of its syrup still clinging to it. Slowly stir it into the cocktail until a slight fog surrounds the glass. This, according to Dave, is the "fermentation," as whiskey eats sugar. *Makes 1*

BIJOU

This version of the classic Bijou was adapted from *Cocktails by "Jimmy" Late of Ciro's* (1930). It also features a cherry for the hungry booze to feast upon.

> 1 pony shot / 30 ml / 1 fl oz green Chartreuse
> 1 pony shot / 30 ml / 1 fl oz dry gin
> 2 tbsp / 1 fl oz red vermouth
> 1 cocktail cherry, preferably Luxardo, as food for the gin
> 1 lemon twist, as garnish

Combine the Chartreuse, gin, and vermouth in a mixing glass half-filled with ice. Let chill about 20 seconds, then julep-strain into a chilled coupe. Garnish with the cherry and the lemon twist, expressing its oil onto the surface, rubbing it onto the rim of the glass, and dropping it in, peel side up. *Makes 1*

THE FRANKLIN MARTINI

You can call this a Dirty Martini, but I prefer its old-fashioned, more demure name.
This is the cocktail FDR chose when it came time to celebrate the repeal of Prohibition.
The reason I resist the more modern moniker is simply that this drink has become a bit
monstrous in its proportions. But pull the olive juice back a bit and let the brine open
your palate to the gentle botanicals in gin and vermouth, and it's a wonderful way to begin
a meal.

2 shots / 90 ml / 3 fl oz dry gin (some prefer vodka)
½ pony shot / 15 ml / ½ fl oz white vermouth
1½ tsp / ¼ fl oz olive juice, such as Dirty Sue or the brine that comes in the
    jar with olives
2 cocktail olives, as garnish

In a mixing glass half-filled with ice, combine the gin (or vodka), vermouth,
and olive juice (or brine). Gently stir until chilled and properly diluted, about
20 seconds. Julep-strain into a chilled cocktail glass and garnish with the
olives. *Makes 1*

DIRTY BIRDY

Here's another briny cocktail to consider, and I've included it in this section because I
really do get the savory allure of a well-made Dirty Martini, especially before dinner. But
Downton Abbey has made a little nip of sherry all the rage lately, so I've reworked the Dirty
Martini using celery-infused vodka and a dry fino-style sherry known as Manzanilla. It
has a complex briny quality that pairs wonderfully with the herbal qualities in this cocktail.
I wonder what the Earl of Grantham would think?

2 pony shots / 60 ml / 2 fl oz Manzanilla sherry
1 pony shot / 30 ml / 1 fl oz celery-infused vodka
    (see Mild-Flavored Vegetable Infusion, page 12)
2 or 3 drops grapefruit bitters
1 cocktail olive, as garnish
1 fresh bay leaf, as garnish

Combine the vodka, sherry, and bitters in a mixing glass half-filled with ice. Gently
stir until chilled and properly diluted, about 20 seconds. Julep-strain into a chilled
cocktail glass. Drop in the olive; slap the bay leaf between the palms of your hands
to bruise it, then drop it on top of the cocktail. *Makes 1*

FRENCH GREEN DRAGON

I don't know if it's really fair of me to call this drink a French Green Dragon. That's the name of an established cocktail of questionable pedigree made of half cognac and half green Chartreuse—a combination that tastes a bit like cough syrup to me. So I decided that this little green monster was in serious need of taming.

First I softened it with Bonal Gentiane-Quina and Armagnac. I typically prefer Armagnac to cognac, especially at the lower end of the price scale. That's because inexpensive cognac can be rather bracing, which may work well for a good stiff belt but wasn't what I needed to smooth the rough edges of this fire-breather. Also, cognacs tend to be mass produced, making many of them one-dimensional, industrial, and boring. An Armagnac at the same price point is likely to be more artisanal.

Once mellowed, this green-tinged tipple has plenty of room for a bit of pizzazz. So I finished it with a dash of bitters, bringing back the moxie that was certainly intended all along.

> 1 shot / 45 ml / 1½ fl oz cognac or Armagnac, preferably Larressingle Armagnac VSOP
> 1 pony shot / 30 ml / 1 fl oz green Chartreuse
> ½ pony shot / 15 ml / ½ fl oz Bonal Gentiane-Quina
> 1 or 2 dashes Bittermens Burlesque Bitters (available online)
>   or Aromatic "House" Bitters (see page 10)

In a mixing glass half-filled with ice, combine the Armagnac, Chartreuse, Bonal, and bitters. Stir until chilled and properly diluted, about 20 seconds. Julep-strain into a chilled coupe or cocktail glass. *Makes 1*

THE WIDOW'S KISS

The Widow's Kiss features another member of the brandy family. It's hugely aromatic and very strong—with complex notes from two of the most venerable French liqueurs out there. Ted Haigh, whose recipe this version closely resembles, credits George Kappeler's *Modern American Drinks* (1895) with the first publication of this fine old Madame.

1 shot / 45 ml / 1½ fl oz apple brandy
½ shot / 22½ ml / ¾ fl oz yellow Chartreuse
½ shot / 22½ ml / ¾ fl oz Benedictine
2 dashes Angostura bitters or Aromatic "House" Bitters (see page 10)
1 cocktail cherry, preferably Luxardo, as garnish

In a mixing glass half-filled with ice, combine the apple brandy, Chartreuse, Benedictine, and bitters. Stir until chilled and properly diluted, about 20 seconds. Julep-strain into a chilled coupe or cocktail glass. Drop the cherry, with some of its syrup still clinging, into the drink. *Makes 1*

INDEX

Absinthe: Dorflinger, 127

The Alexander, 109

Allspice Dram: The Spice Trail, 37

Amaro: Amaro Flip, 115; Barrel-Aged Berlioni, 87; Bitter Beauty, 83; Celery Shrub Cocktail, 53; Chartreuse and the Chocolate Factory, 116; Cool Revival, 111; Dead Glamour, 89; The Fatal Hour, 129; Silk and Gators, 75

Amaro Flip, 115

Anderman, Louis, 125

Anvil, 109

Aperol: Aperol Tequila Swizzle, 91

Aperol Tequila Swizzle, 91

Apple brandy: Autumn Ash, 97; The Widow's Kiss, 135

Aquavit, 123; Celery Shrub Cocktail, 53; Golden Lion, 59; Hair (Raising) Tonic, 123; Scandi Gibson, 37

Armagnac: French Green Dragon, 133

Aromatic "House" Bitters of Your Own, 10

Around the World with Jigger, Beaker, and Flask (1939), 17, 44

Artusi, 89

Autumn Ash, 97

Baker, Charles Henry Jr., 17, 44

Balance of flavor elements, 2

Barrel-Aged Berlioni, 87

Barrel-aged gin, 87

The Beagle, 99

Beer: Charentes Shrub, 85; Smog Cutter, 99

Beet and Juniper Shrub, 11

Beetle Juice, 51

Benedictine: The Widow's Kiss, 135

Berg, Stephan, 23

Better with Bacon, 97

Biancaniello, Matthew, 49

Biarritz Monk, 17

Bijou, 129

Bitter Beauty, 83

Bitter cocktails, 81–92

The Bitter Truth, 23

Bittercube, 33, 57

Bittermens, 37

Bitters, 9–10

Black Pepper Oyster Shooters, 79

Black Salt, 89

Bloody Mary, 69

Bonal Gentiane-Quina: French Green Dragon, 133

Bond, James, 33, 121

Bottoms Up! (1951), 19

Bourbon: Cacao Bourbon, 116; Pork and Beans, 79

Brandy: Top Hat, 33

Breeder's Cup, 49

Brittenham, Taylor, 79

Bullshot, 77

Burning Sensation, 41

Cacao Bourbon, 116

Calvados: Vichy Cycle, 33

Campari: Bitter Beauty, 83; Campari Alexander, 109; The Christopher Oaxacan, 105; Dead Glamour, 89; The Hickory Stick, 103

Canon: Whiskey and Bitters Emporium, 73

Celery Shrub Cocktail, 53

The Chaparral, 101

Charentes Shrub, 85

Chartreuse, green: Bijou, 129; Chartreuse and the Chocolate Factory, 116; Fennel Fizz, 59; French Green Dragon, 133; Greens Fee Fizz, 57; My Word, 19; The Scofflaw, 127

Chartreuse, yellow: Biarritz Monk, 17; "Monk Buck" from Biarritz, 17; Smokejumper, 99; Tom and Daisy, 49; The Widow's Kiss, 135

Chartreuse and the Chocolate Factory, 116

Cherry liqueur: To Hell with Spain #2, 57

The Christopher Oaxacan, 105

Citrus peel, flaming, 125

Citrus syrup, 8–9

Classic Martini, 119

Clove-infused honey syrup, 8

Cocchi Americano: The Christopher Oaxacan, 105; The Grazer's Edge, 63; Neon Rose, 125; Off-

White Negroni, 91; Scandi Gibson, 37; Vesper, 121

Cocktails: bitter, 81–92; herbal, 45–64; preparation, 3–12; presentation, 2–3; rich, 107–16; smoky, 93–106; sour, 13–28; spicy, 29–44; strong, 117–35; umami, 65–80

Cocktails by "Jimmy" Late of Ciro's (1930), 129

Coffee liqueur: Autumn Ash, 97; Black Salt, 89; Pork and Beans, 79

Cognac: Biarritz Monk, 17; French Green Dragon, 133; "Monk Buck" from Biarritz, 17; Silk and Gators, 75; Truffle-Infused Cognac, 73

Coleman, Ada, 92

Cool and Starry, 39

Cool Revival, 111

Craddock, Harry, 92

Crème de cacao: The Alexander, 109; Campari Alexander, 109

Curio, 103

Dead Glamour, 89

Delaney, David, 85

Dickens, Charles, 77

Digestifs, 115

Dill and Lemon Meringue, 111

Dirty Birdy, 131

Dog's Nose, 77

The Dogwood Cocktail Cabin, 35

Donovan, Carol, 21

Dorflinger, 127

Drago Centro, 111

Dry Martini, 119

Eggs, 21

Ehrmann, H. Joseph, 113

El Take It Easy, 95

Elderflower liqueur: Autumn Ash, 97; Golden Ale, 28; Sungold Zinger, 71

Elixir, 113

Ensslin, Hugo, 109

Equipment, 3–5

Extra-Dry Martini, 119

The Fatal Hour, 129

Fennel Fizz, 59

Fernet-Branca: Bitter Beauty, 83; Black Salt, 89; Hanky Panky, 92; The Hickory Stick, 103

Fleming, Ian, 33, 121

Fortuna, Adam, 89

The Franklin Martini, 131

French Green Dragon, 133

Gall, Chris, 87

Galliano: Golden Lion, 59

Garden Party Punch, 25

Genever, 44; Warm Cardigan, 43

Gentian liqueur: Off-White Negoroni, 91

Gibson, 121

Gibson, Charles Dana, 121

Gin, 44, 87; The Alexander, 109; Barrel-Aged Berlioni, 87; Beetle Juice, 51; Bijou, 129; Bitter Beauty, 83; Breeder's Cup, 49; Classic Martini, 119; Dog's Nose, 77; Dorflinger, 127; Dry Martini, 119; Extra-Dry Martini, 119; The Franklin Martini, 131; Garden Party Punch, 25; Gibson, 121; Green Tea

Gimlet, 23; Greens Fee Fizz, 57; Hanky Panky, 92; Neon Rose, 125; "Perfect" Martini, 119; Pimm's Cup Up, 55; Pink Peppercorn Hot Gin Sling, 43; Rhubarb Rosemary Flip, 21; Salad Bowl Gin and Tonic, 61; A Savory Cocktail, 53; Smokejumper, 99; Smoky Martini, 119; The Spice Trail, 37; Sungold Zinger, 71; Tartufo, 73; Truffle-Infused Cognac, 73; types, 44, 87; Vesper, 121

Ginger and black pepper agave syrup, 7–8

Ginger beer: Cool and Starry, 39

Ginger liqueur: Pimm's Cup Up, 55; Yuzu Sour, 27

Glasser, Avery, 37

Glasses, "rinsing," 57, 116

Glassware, 2–3

Golden Ale, 28

Golden Lion, 59

The Grazer's Edge, 63

Green Gargoyle, 31

Green Tea Gimlet, 23

Greenbaum, Dan, 99

Greens Fee Fizz, 57

Grier, Jacob, 59, 99

The Guayabera, 113

Habanero agave syrup, 8

Haigh, Ted, 92, 135

Hair (Raising) Tonic, 123

Hakkinen, Erik, 33

Hanky Panky, 92

Hazard, Nathan, 25, 91, 105

The Hearty Boys, 21

Hemingway, Ernest, 15

Herbal cocktails, 45–64

Heugel, Bobby, 109
The Hickory Stick, 103
Holland Razor Blade, 44
Hollywood Roosevelt Hotel's
    Library Bar, 49
Homemade Spicy Dill Pickles
    and Brine, 80; Pickleback
    (Make Mine a Double),
    80
Hotchner, A. E., 15
"House" Bitters, 10
House Spirits Distillery, 53

Ice, 5
Infusions, 11–12
Ink restaurant, 28
Islay whisky: Penicillin
    Cocktail, 106

Kappeler, George, 135
Kina Lillet, 121
Koplowitz, Ira, 33, 57
Kümmel: Top Hat, 33; Vichy
    Cycle, 33

Lapsang souchong syrup, 99
Lillet Blanc, 121
Lillet Rose: Garden Party
    Punch, 25
Linie aquavit: Hair (Raising)
    Tonic, 123
London Dry Gin, 44
The Long Goodbye, 95

Maison Premiere, 103
Malt whisky. See Whiskey/
    whisky
Mandeville, Jaymee, 111
Maraschino liqueur: Moonlit
    Night, 23; My Word,
    19; Papa Hemingway
    Daiquiri, 15; Top Hat, 33
Mason jars, 63
Measurements, 6

Meehan, Jim, 87
Metrovino, 59
Mezcal blanco, 95; The
    Christopher Oaxacan,
    105; The Long Goodbye,
    95; Rickey Oaxaqueña,
    105; Smog Cutter, 99
Mezcal reposado: The
    Chaparral, 101
Mlynarczyk, Gabriella, 28
Modern American Drinks (1895),
    135
Monteiro, Gonçalo de Sousa,
    87
"Monk Buck" from Biarritz,
    17
Moonlit Night, 23
My Word, 19

Neon Rose, 125
Nicholson, Linda Miller, 31
North Shore Distillery, 59

Off-White Negroni, 91
Old Hickory, 103
Old Tom Gin, 44; Hair
    (Raising) Tonic, 123;
    My Word, 19; Off-White
    Negroni, 91; Tom and
    Daisy, 49
The Old Waldorf-Astoria Bar Book
    (1935), 127
Oleo-saccharum (syrup), 9
Owens, Travis, 103, 105

Papa Hemingway Daiquiri,
    15
The PDT Cocktail Book, 87
Penicillin Cocktail, 106
"Perfect" Martini, 119
Picasso, Pablo, 91
Pickleback (Make Mine a
    Double), 80
Pimm's Cup Up, 55

Pimm's No. 1: Pimm's Cup
    Up, 55
Pineapple Rosemary Shrub,
    10–11
Pineau des Charentes:
    Charentes Shrub, 85
The Pickwick Papers, 77
Pink Peppercorn Hot Gin
    Sling, 43
Pisco: Yuzu Sour, 27
Plymouth Dry Gin, 44
Porcini mushroom powder,
    77
Pork and Beans, 79
Porter, Jay, 95
Porter: Dog's Nose, 77
Prichard, Benjamin, 116

Range, 71
Ray's and Stark Bar, 75
Recipes for Mixed Drinks (1917),
    109
Rhubarb Rosemary Flip, 21
Rich cocktails, 107–16
Rickey Oaxaqueña, 105
Roosevelt, Franklin D., 131
Ross, Sam, 106
Rum: Cool and Starry,
    39; Papa Hemingway
    Daiquiri, 15; Rum-
    Muddled Diplomat, 39
Rum-Muddled Diplomat,
    39
Rye: Better with Bacon,
    97; Black Salt, 89; Cool
    Revival, 111; The Fatal
    Hour, 129; The Scofflaw,
    127

Spice Trail, 37
Salad Bowl Gin and Tonic,
    61
Sanguinetti, Paul, 75
Saucier, Ted, 19

A Savory Cocktail, 53

Savory Tomato Juice, 67: Black Pepper Oyster Shooters, 79; Bloody Mary, 69

Savoy Cocktail Book (1930), 92

Savoy Hotel's American Bar, 92

Scandi Gibson, 37

Scarborough Fair, 61

Schwartz, Jeremy, 79

The Scofflaw, 127

Scotch. *See* Whiskey/whisky

Shaken vs. stirred, 5–6

Sherry, 75; Dirty Birdy, 131; Silk and Gators, 75

Shrubs (drinking vinegars), 10–11

Silk and Gators, 75

Simple syrup, 6

Smog Cutter, 99

Smokejumper, 99

Smoky cocktails, 93–106

Smoky Martini, 119

Sour cocktails, 13–28

The Spice Trail, 37

Spicy cocktails, 29–44

Stenson, Murray, 19, 33

Stirred vs. shaken, 5–6

Strong cocktails, 117–35

Sungold Zinger, 71

Suze: Off-White Negroni, 91

Syrups, 6–9

Tartufo, 73

Techniques, 5–6: flaming citrus peel, 125; rinsing glass, 57, 116; shaking vs. stirring, 5–6

Tequila blanco: Aperol Tequila Swizzle, 91; The Chaparral, 101; Green Gargoyle, 31; Moonlit Night, 23

Tequila reposado: Burning Sensation, 41; Dead Glamour, 89

Thai Bird Chile Kamikaze, 41

This Feeling of Joy, 64

To Hell with Spain #2, 57

Tom and Daisy, 49

Tools, 3–5

Top Hat, 33

Triple C Collins, 47

Truffle-honey syrup, 73

Truffle-Infused Cognac, 73

Truffles, 73

Umami cocktails, 65–80

Vermouth, red: Bijou, 129; The Christopher Oaxacan, 105; Hanky Panky, 92; The Hickory Stick, 103; Old Hickory, 103; "Perfect" Martini, 119; A Savory Cocktail, 53; Silk and Gators, 75; The Spice Trail, 37; To Hell with Spain #2, 57

Vermouth, white: Barrel-Aged Berlioni, 87; Bitter Beauty, 83; Classic Martini, 119; Dry Martini, 119; Extra-Dry Martini, 119; The Franklin Martini, 131; Gibson, 121; Golden Lion, 59; The Hickory Stick, 103; Old Hickory, 103; "Perfect" Martini, 119; Scarborough Fair, 61; The Scofflaw, 127; Smoky Martini, 119; Vichy Cycle, 33

Vesper, 121

Vichy Cycle, 33

Villains Tavern, 129

Vintage Spirits and Forgotten Cocktails (2004, 2009), 92

Violet liqueur: Moonlit Night, 23

Vodka: Beetle Juice, 51; Black Pepper Oyster Shooters, 79; Bloody Mary, 69; Bullshot, 77; Dirty Birdy, 131; Fennel Fizz, 59; The Franklin Martini, 131; Golden Ale, 28; The Grazer's Edge, 63; The Guayabera, 113; Scarborough Fair, 61; Thai Bird Chile Kamikaze, 41; This Feeling of Joy, 64; Triple C Collins, 47; Vesper, 121; Winter Squash, 35

Warm Cardigan, 43

West Restaurant + Bar, 116

Whiskey/whisky, 97; Autumn Ash, 97; Penicillin cocktail, 106; Pickleback (Make Mine a Double), 80; Smoky Martini, 119

Whitton, Dave, 129

The Widow's Kiss, 135

Wilson, Jason, 127

Wilson, Phoebe, 35

Windak, Andy, 53

Winter Squash, 35

Wolowidnyk, David, 116

Yuzu juice, 27; Cool Revival, 111; Golden Ale, 28; Yuzu Sour, 27

Yuzu Sour, 27

Zig Zag Café, 19, 33

Žubrówka vodka, 64

ACKNOWLEDGMENTS

There are many people to thank, starting with the many bartenders whose paths I've crossed. I'm most grateful to those who have made unique contributions to this book. Their dedication to their craft helped guide me on a long and enjoyable journey into the art of the cocktail.

I'm not a bartender myself. My interest stems from a love of food and a love of communicating that love, which led to my blog *Sippity Sup—Serious Fun Food*. On its face, blogging seems a rather solitary activity. In fact, that's one of the things that drew me to it. I often sit alone in my bathrobe and "work." The cloistered aspect still appeals to me, but the more involved I get in blogging, the more I see how deeply communal it really is. So I need to thank the countless other bloggers who through example and shared passion taught me how to express myself in that very baffling medium called the blogosphere.

Another book and another big thank-you to my brother, Grant Henry, who collaborated on the wine pairings in my book *Savory Pies*. He lends his expertise again in this book, with an explanation on sherry and all its subtleties (see page 75).

Thanks also to the hardworking folks at Ulysses Press. Particularly Katherine Furman and Keith Riegert, who gave me the freedom I needed to develop this subject. In many ways *Savory Cocktails* breaks new ground, and I appreciate their patience as I mixed and re-mixed cocktails in the effort to define the genre for myself.

Lastly, my partner, Ken, is responsible for much of the look of this book. His impeccable taste and design sense helped me see this book in my mind so that it actually became possible to write it.

ABOUT THE AUTHOR

GREG HENRY is a professional photographer and the author of *Savory Pies* (Ulysses Press). He also writes the food blog *Sippity Sup—Serious Fun Food*. He's led cooking demonstrations in Panama and Costa Rica, and has traveled as far and wide as Norway and Alaska to promote culinary travel. He's been featured in *Food & Wine* magazine, the *Los Angeles Times*, the *Today* show online, and *Saveur* magazine's "Best of the Web." Greg also co-hosts The Table Set podcast, which was named one of *LA Weekly*'s 5 favorite podcasts for food lovers. It can be downloaded on iTunes or at Homefries Podcast Network. Greg has lived in Los Angeles with his partner Ken for over 20 years. Entertaining friends at home is a passion of his and the genesis for this book.